HERITAGE OF IRELAND

EXECUTIVE EDITOR Julian Brown
EDITOR Karen O'Grady
ART DIRECTOR Keith Martin
SENIOR DESIGNER Geoff Borin
DESIGN Geoff Fennell
PRODUCTION Julie Hadingham
PICTURE RESEARCH Charlotte Deane

First published in Great Britain in 1998 by Hamlyn,
a division of Octopus Publishing Group Ltd

This 2001 edition published by Chancellor Press,
an imprint of Bounty Books, a division of
Octopus Publishing Group Ltd,
2-4 Heron Quays, London E14 4JP

Copyright © Octopus Publishing Group Ltd 1998

ISBN 0 7537 0556 7

A catalogue record for this book is
available from the British Library

Produced by Toppan
Printed in China

HERITAGE OF IRELAND

A HISTORY OF IRELAND & ITS PEOPLE

NATHANIEL HARRIS

hamlyn

CONTENTS

INTRODUCTION

'IT IS THE BEAUTY OF IRELAND THAT HAS MADE US WHAT WE ARE', DECLARED THE PLAYWRIGHT GEORGE BERNARD SHAW. IF THAT IS SO, IRELAND'S MISTY MOUNTAINS, SHIMMERING LAKES AND GREEN-MANTLED LAND MUST POSSESS SOME SPECIAL MAGIC; FOR THERE IS NOWHERE LIKE IRELAND AND NO PEOPLE QUITE LIKE THE IRISH.

Among other things they are indomitable: seven hundred years of occupation failed to refashion them in the image of their British neighbours, and as brilliant writers and talkers they have appropriated rather than capitulated to the English language.

Nevertheless a keen sense of history is a vital element in the Irish identity. When the purpose of Ireland's Stone Age monuments had long been forgotten, the Irish imagination brought them back into folk-consciousness, as landmarks said to have figured in much later tales; and so, in the great myth-cycles of the pagan Celts, openings in burial mounds were believed to be entrances to the underworld, and the stone skeletons of ancient tombs became the beds of tragic lovers.

The culture of these Celtic Irish – warriors, craftsmen and bards – continued to flourish after most of Celtic Europe had succumbed to the expanding Roman Empire. Skilfully wrought metalwork, and a distinctive Celtic style of decoration, survived into the Middle Ages and profoundly influenced other arts – including the art of the book, introduced by Christianity. The triumph of the new faith in the 5th-6th centuries did not end the Celtic warrior tradition, but it did create the band of 'scholars and saints' for whom Ireland became famous. Irish evangelists worked to convert the Scots, the English, and heathens even further afield, while monks in Ireland itself were preserving the rudiments of a foundering European civilization by copying and studying ancient texts. Historically these were their greatest achievements; but visually there is nothing to compare with their fashioning of wonderful illuminated manuscripts such as the Book of Kells, which rank among the masterpieces of European art.

Ireland's monastic culture waxed and waned, and the invaders came: Vikings from Scandinavia, followed by conqueror-settlers from the island next door. These newcomers were known under different names – Normans or English or British – but pursued the same policy of domination, modified only by their tendency to take on local colour and become 'more Irish than the Irish'.

The long and tangled relationship that ensued is one of the themes of this book. But alongside the dramatic, too often tragic narrative of Irish history must be set the many colourful and creative elements of Ireland's past: the lively society, the stirring tales, the legacy of fine monuments and buildings, the art and literature of a great and gifted people. Finally there is contemporary Ireland, a country not completely liberated from the ghosts of the past, but still welcoming, beautiful, creative and, increasingly, forward- and outward-looking.

THE LAND

LEFT: MacGillycuddy's Reeks, County Kerry
RIGHT: The Caha Mountains, County Cork

THE BLASKET ISLANDS FROM Coomeenoole beach, County Kerry

A GREEN LAND OF SPARKLING
   LAKES AND RIVERS,
BOGS AND MISTY MOUNTAINS:
   IRELAND IS ALL OF THESE,
BUT VERY MUCH MORE BESIDES

ATLANTIC ISLAND

IRELAND IS EUROPE'S WESTERN OUTPOST, FRONTING THE VASTNESS OF THE ATLANTIC. THIS HAS BEEN ONE OF THE CENTRAL FACTS OF ITS HISTORY.

For centuries, until the discovery of the Americas, the island was regarded as a remote spot on the edge of the inhabited world, and new ideas and technologies did generally reach it very late – which only makes the distinctive Irish contribution to civilization seem all the more remarkable.

Other accidents of geography and climate were equally important in shaping Ireland's destiny. For all its ferocity, the ocean played a crucial role in the making of the land, bringing to its shores the warm currents that helped to make it mild, moist and green. And, more ambiguously, the island's proximity to its more resource-rich neighbour, Britain, influenced the entire course of Irish history for good and ill; although the political outcome has more often than not been unfavourable to Ireland, warriors and missionaries, creators and destroyers, passed in both directions across the sea.

The shape of the land is unusual. Essentially it consists of a rolling, fertile area, the Central Lowlands, which is surrounded by low ranges of hills and mountains; the very highest point on the island, in Macgillycuddy's Reeks, stands a mere 1040 metres above sea level. The one long break in the ranges occurs in the east, where the lowlands extend as far as the coast, from Dublin to Dundalk Bay – an all-too-helpful entry-point for invaders and settlers.

A WATERSIDE SCENE IN CONNEMARA, COUNTY GALWAY. DESPITE ITS TRANQUIL APPEARANCE, THIS IS WILD, LONELY COUNTRY, DOTTED WITH SMALL, LAKES AND COVERED WITH BOGLAND; THE ECOLOGICAL VALUE OF THE AREA HAS BEEN RECOGNISED BY THE CREATION OF THE CONNEMARA NATIONAL PARK

However, much of Ireland's special character derives from the network of rivers and lakes (known as loughs) which divide up the land. The river Shannon rises modestly out of a hole called the Shannon Pot in County Cavan, but then flows on and on until it empties into the sea some 400 kilometres away in the far south-west. It is the longest river not only in Ireland but in the British Isles; and, similarly, Lough Neagh, almost 400 square kilometres in area, is the biggest lake. The land is tamer than was once the case: the forests have long disappeared, and even Ireland's famous peat bogs are much diminished. But although industries, cities and 'post-industrial' enterprises have made their mark on the landscape, Ireland remains an extraordinarily spacious place, full of pleasant small towns and villages, mansions and ruins, that complement rather than dominate the peaceful farmlands and magnificently varied scenery.

A PEACEFUL SCENE ON THE RIVER BANN at Coleraine, close to its exit into the sea on the rugged far northern coast of Ireland. In its course the Bann passes through landscape of great variety, rising in the Mourne Mountains and pouring in and out of Lough Neagh, the largest lake in the British Isles

THE TWELVE BENS ARE A DRAMATIC SERIES OF PEAKS IN THE CENTRE OF CONNEMARA; THE HIGHEST, BENBAUN, RISES TO 730 METRES. EVEN NOW, THE HEART OF THE TWELVE BENS IS ONLY ACCESSIBLE BY A FEW NARROW TRACKS, AND CONSIDERABLE FORTITUDE IS STILL REQUIRED TO SCALE THEIR BOGGY SLOPES. IRONICALLY, THE UNSPOILED LOVELINESS OF CONNEMARA OWES MUCH TO ITS REMOTENESS AND LACK OF FERTILE SOIL

THE FOUR PROVINCES

IRELAND IS VERY OFTEN BEEN DESCRIBED IN TERMS OF
ITS FOUR HISTORIC PROVINCES: ULSTER IN THE NORTH,
LEINSTER IN THE EAST AND CENTRE, MUNSTER IN THE
SOUTH-WEST, AND IN THE FAR WEST, CONNAUGHT,
OR CONNACHT.

ONE OF ULSTER'S GEMS THE MOURNE
MOUNTAINS 'GO DOWN TO THE SEA' (IN THE
WORDS OF AN OLD SONG) ON THE EAST COAST.
THEIR IMPRESSIVE PURPLE SLOPES CREATE A GENTLER,
MORE TRANQUIL ATMOSPHERE THAN THAT OF THEIR
SPECTACULARLY RUGGED RIVALS IN THE WEST

Meath (centre-north) was in earlier times
one of the 'Five Fifths' of Ireland, but now
forms part of Leinster. The four-way division is
a convenient one, since it does in a general way
correspond to regions whose landscape and
history differ from one another.

In traditional usage Ulster consists of nine
counties, although the word is sometimes used to describe the six that
are currently part of the United Kingdom. Ancient Ulster was a Gaelic
warrior kingdom, whose heroes and rulers were celebrated in Ireland's
great mythological cycles. Stories and legends haunt many of its impressive natural features, which include Lough Neagh, the glens of Antrim,
the Mountains of Mourne, the astonishing Giant's Causeway, and Donegal, with its wild coastline, sea loughs, and bleakly lovely landscape.

In the southern counties of Ulster, the terrain is characterized by
huge numbers of low, rounded hills known as drumlins, created by the
glaciers of the last Ice Age. Further south lies Leinster, which takes in the

capital of the Republic of Ireland, Dublin, as well as the populous and popular east and south-east coasts and the Central Lowlands, an area of dairy farms, market towns, peat bogs, and tranquil glens and lakes.

The open coastal plain and its rivers – Dublin's Liffey, the Boyne and the Bann – have always been inviting to outsiders and natural centres for the exercise of pride and power. The Neolithic Irish erected gigantic tombs in the valley of the Boyne; not far away, on the Hill of Tara, the high kings of Celtic Ireland were crowned; and on the Boyne itself, at Trim, the Normans built the mightiest of their Irish castles. Dublin and the area surrounding it easily have the longest continuous history of English occupation; once known as 'the Pale', it was held for the Crown even during the late Middle Ages, when the English grip on Ireland was at its weakest. To the south lie the Wicklow Mountains, gold-bearing in prehistoric times, later bandit-infested, but nowadays the delight of moorland walkers and visitors who tour the ancient monastic buildings of Glendalough.

The Shannon forms the long western boundary between Leinster and Connaught. The river, flowing south through a series of loughs, is in effect a separate eco-world; and with the Erne, which rises not far from the Shannon Pot in Cavan and flows north-west through Donegal, it constitutes Ireland's most impressive lake and river system. At various times a highway and a military frontier, the

WATERFALL AT GLENMACNASS, one of many exhilarating sights in the Wicklow Mountains just south of Dublin, famous alike for their peaks and glens, wildlife and religious remains. Their proximity to the capital makes the Wicklows a popular refuge for weekend ramblers and excursionists

THE SEA-WORN COASTLINE OF COUNTY DONEGAL, CELEBRATED FOR ITS IRREGULAR PENINSULAS, LARGE BAYS AND DEEP INLETS. HIGHLY DISTINCTIVE IN CHARACTER, DONEGAL IS THE WESTERNMOST COUNTY OF ULSTER AND THE NORTHERNMOST PART OF THE IRISH REPUBLIC

Shannon runs beside many places of historical importance, among them Clonmacnoise, with its extraordinary concentration of ecclesiastical remains, and the towns of Athlone and Limerick, where decisive engagements took place during the wars of the 17th century.

Across the river lies the West of Ireland, most of it within the province of Connaught. For many people – Irish people as well as outsiders – this is Ireland at its most romantic. In legend, Connaught was once a powerful kingdom, vying with Ulster for supremacy. But later, when most of the traditional gentry lost their lands, they were given only one choice by an implacable Oliver Cromwell – 'Hell or Connaught!' And as the English language spread across Ireland, the West became the home of the shrinking Gaeltacht, the areas where Gaelic was still the tongue of the people.

THE SPECTACULAR CLIFFS OF MOHER.
THESE ARE MAGNIFICENT NATURAL RUINS ON THE COAST OF COUNTY CLARE, APPARENTLY INDESTRUCTIBLE BUT IN FACT CRUMBLING INTO THE ATLANTIC UNDER THE MERCILESS IMPACT OF WIND, RAIN AND WAVES

Many parts of this land are both bleak and beautiful. Ceaselessly wave-battered, the spectacular western coastline has been worn into a ragged pattern of promontories and inlets. Beyond are the groups of little offshore islands, hostages to the Atlantic, where life is so hard that some have been abandoned within living memory – but not so the Aran Islands, with their immense and mysterious prehistoric fortifications; their way of life, made famous in literature and film, is sustained – and threatened – by tourism.

On the mainland, Sligo is rich in history, but is now seen above all as 'Yeats country'; and it is true that names such as Ben Bulben and Innisfree instantly bring the poet to mind. To the south, Galway is wilder and, in places, more desolate; in the western part of the county, Connemara now boasts a National Park to preserve its beautiful moorland, lakes and streams. Its stones are among the most striking features of County Clare: the Burren, limestone upland on which Neolithic dolmens celebrate the anciently dead, and brilliant flowers appear in the spring; and the awe-inspiring Cliffs of Moher.

Although behind the Shannon, Clare is technically part of Munster; but most of this south-western province has a generally milder air. In large part this is created by the Gulf Stream, which makes it possible to grow palms and other semi-tropical plants. Tourists have responded to the climate, to scenery such as the Ring of Kerry and the lakes of Killarney, and to the lively cities of Limerick, Cork and Waterford. Meanwhile the Rock of Cashel and the Blarney Stone (Castle Blarney, County Cork) remind us that, as in every part of Ireland, the past is very much alive.

INISHEER, SMALLEST OF THE ARAN ISLANDS.
The three islands are little more than stone outcrops
at the mouth of Galway Bay, and their primitive way
of life has fascinated both authors (J.M. Synge) and
film makers (Robert Flaherty). Any soil on the islands
had to be transferred from the mainland or scraped
from cracks in the rocks and fertilized with seaweed;
and the little fields are still divided up by weaving,
maze-like drystone walls. The islanders eked out a
living by fishing and weaving (Aran sweaters have
become famous) until tourism improved their fortunes

STORM CLOUDS OVER LOUGH CONN, A LARGE LAKE IN THE HEART OF COUNTY
MAYO; ALONG WITH THE ADJACENT LOUGH CULLIN, IT IS A NOTABLE BEAUTY SPOT AND
ALSO A FAVOURED HAUNT OF ANGLERS. THE RUINS OF 15TH CENTURY ERREW ABBEY STAND
ON A LONG TONGUE OF LAND THRUSTING OUT INTO THE WATER

THE ISLAND'S PAST

LEFT: The Mourne Mountains, County Down
RIGHT: Imaginary portrait of Saint Patrick

LEFT: Emigrant ship leaving Belfast, by John Glen Wilson

WARLIKE CELTS, CHRISTIAN SAINTS,
AND SCHOLARS, PATRICIANS
AND PEASANTS, REBELS AND EXILES;
IRELAND'S TURBULENT HISTORY HAS
PROVIDED A GREAT VARIETY OF ROLES
FOR HER PEOPLE

17

THE FIRST IRISH

HUMAN BEINGS WERE LATE IN COMING TO IRELAND. LIKE THE OTHER PARTS OF NORTHERN EUROPE, MOST OF THE IRISH LANDSCAPE WAS A FROZEN AND BARREN WILDERNESS FOR THE ONE-AND-A-HALF MILLION YEARS OF THE LAST GREAT ICE AGE.

A GREAT PASSAGE TOMB AT LOUGHCREW, COUNTY MEATH. FOUR AND A HALF THOUSAND YEARS OLD, THESE MIGHTY PREHISTORIC MOUNDS HAVE BEEN COMPARED WITH THE EGYPTIAN PYRAMIDS

Then, as temperatures rose and the ice retreated, Ireland emerged as part of the European mainland, linked by land bridges to Britain, which was in turn attached to the Continent. Plants and creatures colonized them until about 8000 BC, when melting ice raised the sea levels and the bridges linking Ireland and Britain disappeared.

Some fauna and flora failed to reach Ireland before the waters rose – notably the snake, although legend was later to credit St Patrick with banishing it. If any human beings were among the fauna that crossed to Ireland by land, they have left no discernable traces. The earliest known Irish must have arrived in primitive boats, probably from south-west Scotland; visible from Scotland's Mull of Kintyre, the Irish coast is a mere twenty kilometres away, making possible a two-way traffic that has affected the history of both countries. Arriving in Ireland at some time after 8000 BC, these Stone Age hunters, fishers and food-gatherers worked their way south over the millennia, following the banks of Ireland's rivers and lakes. Their way of life changed little until about 4000 BC, when a new and more advanced culture appeared, possibly brought in by outsiders.

This culture was Neolithic – that is, one that still involved the use of stone tools and weapons, but was based on farming instead of hunting or simply gathering food. Clearing the land, sowing seeds and harvesting

INTRICATE DECORATION, cut into a stone slab above the burial chamber of the great mound at Newgrange. A remarkably similar decorative impulse persisted in Ireland for millennia

crops, stock-raising and pottery-making became the prime constituents of a new way of life, pioneered several thousand years earlier in the Near East. Since the Neolithic Irish knew nothing of writing, we have no unambiguous evidence about their thoughts and feelings; but their ability to work together on a large scale, and their preoccupation with death and eternity, are unmistakably attested to by the stupendous monuments they left behind them to honour or appease the dead. Above all there are the great tomb mounds (barrows), dating from about 3000 BC, of which the most celebrated are Knowth, Dowth and Newgrange in the Boyne Valley. Once regarded as barbaric imitations of the Giza pyramids of ancient Egypt, these Irish 'passage tombs' are now known to be older than the pyramids and are admired accordingly.

A new phase of Irish prehistory began with the introduction of metalworking around 2000 BC; knowledge of metals may have been brought by settlers or invaders, but may equally well have been acquired through trade. As a result, copper and gold were mined, smelted and worked into useful and beautiful objects, and Ireland began to play a significant role in the international economy. New customs, such as the erection of stone circles, suggest that this was a period of significant cultural development. The end of the Bronze Age roughly coincided with the emergence of a distinctively Celtic Irish society.

DOLMENS OR PORTAL TOMBS, ARE FOUND ALL OVER IRELAND. THEY NOW CONSIST OF TWO OR THREE UPRIGHT STONES WHICH SUPPORT A LARGE, FLAT 'CAPSTONE'; BUT ORIGINALLY THE SIDES WOULD HAVE BEEN FILLED IN WITH EARTH TO FORM A MOUND. THIS EXAMPLE, STANDING ON THE STONY PLATEAU OF THE BURREN (COUNTY CLARE), IS PARTICULARLY DRAMATIC

CELTIC KINGDOMS

IRELAND'S FIRST WRITTEN RECORDS DATE FROM THE 7TH CENTURY AD, PERHAPS A THOUSAND YEARS AFTER THE CELTS CAME TO DOMINATE IT.

So it is not surprising that scholars are still debating whether the Celts introduced iron technology when they arrived as invaders or settlers – or, for that matter, whether their 'arrival' represented anything more than the development in Ireland of a culture that had already spread across northern Europe from Britain to the Balkans.

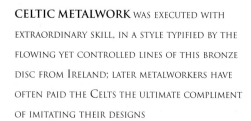

The most common view is that the Celts moved into Ireland at some time after 500 BC, possibly in several waves, and that they brought with them the Gaelic language, a social order based on warrior values, and a religion involving features such as sacred groves, druids (priests), a severed-head cult and human sacrifice.

In view of their later history, it seems almost certain that they established dozens of petty kingdoms, or *tuatha*, and fought endlessly among themselves; if the great cycles of myths are to be believed, Celtic pride, honour and passion were regular sources of epic mayhem. Archaeological excavations confirm the widespread use of hill forts, island strongholds and other means of defence, although similar evidence of Iron Age insecurity is also found in other lands. Over the centuries there was a tendency for the petty kings to become subject to provincial overlords, and by about AD 1000 the division of Ireland into the Five Fifths (Ulster, Meath, Leinster, Munster, Connaught) was probably well established. From the 8th century AD one or another of these provincial kings claimed to be 'high king' of Ireland, but the title was rarely accepted everywhere and carried more prestige than power.

CELTIC METALWORK WAS EXECUTED WITH EXTRAORDINARY SKILL, IN A STYLE TYPIFIED BY THE FLOWING YET CONTROLLED LINES OF THIS BRONZE DISC FROM IRELAND; LATER METALWORKERS HAVE OFTEN PAID THE CELTS THE ULTIMATE COMPLIMENT OF IMITATING THEIR DESIGNS

During the 1st century AD, the Romans conquered most of Celtic Britain (present-day England and Wales, and southern Scotland). Until recently it was believed that Ireland remained undisturbed, but excavations in the 1990s uncovered a large fort of the Roman type on the coast of Drumanagh, north of Dublin. The proper interpretation of the finds is still a matter of controversy, but at the very least they suggest that Roman influence on Celtic Ireland was more substantial than has sometimes been admitted.

Coins from the Drumanagh site suggest that it dates from the 2nd century AD, when the Roman Empire was at the height of its power and prosperity under the Antonines. Within a century, Rome was facing difficulties and Latin writers were describing the increasingly frequent

raids launched by the warlike Irish on the coasts of Britain. In time the Irish established colonies in Wales, Devon and Cornwall, and in the 5th century the Irish of Dal Riata in the north-east began to cross into Argyll; these invaders would eventually absorb the native Picts and found the kingdom of Scotland.

It was early in the 5th century that the last Roman legions left Britain. The Empire rapidly disintegrated all over the West, to be replaced by new barbarian kingdoms. Britain's Romanized culture and urban way of life went into decline; yet Roman and British influence was soon felt much more powerfully than ever in Ireland, as the Christian religion took hold there.

CELTIC WARFARE WAS A SERIOUS BUSINESS, TO JUDGE BY THE NUMBER AND CHARACTER OF IRISH DEFENSIVE ARRANGEMENTS. EVEN THE TINY, INFERTILE ARAN ISLANDS WERE FORTIFIED AS IF IN PREPARATION FOR LIFE-AND-DEATH STRUGGLES. IN FACT DUN AENGHUS ON INISHMORE, SHOWN HERE, IS ONE OF THE MOST IMPRESSIVE OF ALL IRON AGE FORTS, WITH THREE LINES OF RAMPARTS BACKING ON TO SHEER CLIFFS STANDING ABOVE THE SEA

THE COMING OF CHRISTIANITY

CHRISTIANITY ALMOST CERTAINLY REACHED IRELAND SOMETIME DURING THE 4TH CENTURY AD, FOLLOWING THE CONVERSION OF NEIGHBOURING BRITAIN, WHICH WAS AT THAT TIME STILL UNDER ROMAN RULE.

BEEHIVE HUTS, OR CLOCHANS, ON THE ISLAND OF SKELLIG MICHAEL, OFF THE SOUTH-WEST COAST. THEY ONCE HOUSED MONKS WHO, PERHAPS INSPIRED BY EARLY CHRISTIAN HERMITS IN EGYPT, SOUGHT OUT RE-MOTE PLACES IN WHICH TO FOLLOW THE SPIRITUAL LIFE

It was only a little later, in 431, that Pope Celestine I dispatched a missionary named Palladius as bishop to combat heresy among 'the Irish believing in Christ', who were presumably quite numerous. The conversion of the entire community was probably a long-drawn-

out process, but tradition has simplified it by giving all the credit to St Patrick. Ireland's patron saint was actually a Romanized Briton. Kidnapped by Irish pirates when he was sixteen, Patrick worked for six years as a herder before escaping and making his way back to Britain. His faith strengthened by his experiences, he trained for the priesthood and in

432 (says tradition) he returned to Ireland to preach the Gospel – evidently with success, although remarkably little is known of his activities other than the few biographical details given in the *Confession*, a statement written by Patrick in answer to some of his critics.

From the 6th century onwards, Irish Christianity flourished mightily. Though local rulers promoted the new religion, neither they nor their subjects easily gave up old habits; but within the Church itself, an intense devotion produced an extraordinary number of heroic saints, scholars and solitaries. Developing its own distinctive character, the Celtic Church was more loosely organized than its Roman parent. Gifted individual churchmen and great monasteries played an outstanding role. Some of the monasteries, patronized by local rulers, became wealthy and influential, but many individuals and groups rejected the world, seeking out bleak and remote places in which to work and worship. The search was not confined to Ireland itself, but impelled monks to settle Iceland before the Vikings even found it; and it sent the 6th-century St Brendan, Abbot of Clonfert, on a long voyage that some believe to have ended on the coast of America!

THE VOYAGE OF ST BRENDAN. In this medieval manuscript, the saint and his unlucky companions are borne up by a sea monster. St Brendan was a real person who lived in the 6th century and founded the monastery of Clonfert. He owes his European fame to a much-translated 10th-century book Brendan's Voyage, in which he discovers an Eden-like land of promise somewhere in the Atlantic

However, Ireland's contributions to European civilization were of a more tangible nature. With the Roman world in ruins and literacy in retreat, the monasteries of the newly literate Irish became sanctuaries of learning where precious texts were preserved and disseminated by copying. The laws, annals and myths of Celtic society were also rescued from oblivion, and the making of books – masterpieces such as the Book of Durrow and the Book of Kells – became an art as well as an act of piety.

Abroad, Irish missionaries were extraordinarily active. In about 563 St Columba, or Colmcille, founded a monastery on the island of Iona, off the Scottish coast. This became the base for the conversion of the Picts and a celebrated re-evangelization of northern Britain, spearheaded by St. Aidan from the monastery he founded on the island of Lindisfarne. Further afield, St Columba's near-namesake, St Columban, was only the most famous of many intrepid Irish missionaries who journeyed tirelessly over western and central Europe; as well as saving souls, they founded monasteries that became famous and settlements that often grew into cities. 'The Golden Age of Irish Christianity' may be a cliché, but it is certainly not an exaggeration.

INVADERS

WHILE EUROPE WAS BATTERED BY WAVE AFTER WAVE OF 'BARBARIAN' OUTSIDERS, IRELAND ENJOYED A RELATIVE PEACE THAT MADE IT POSSIBLE FOR HER TO BECOME A LAND OF SAINTS AND SCHOLARS.

The peace was only relative, since the great and small rulers of the Five Fifths continued to feud and fight, even after the descendants of Nial of the Nine Hostages, king of Meath, made good their claim to be high kings of Ireland.

In practice the high king's authority was extremely limited, and any prospect of political unification became even more remote when Ireland began to experience the kind of 'barbarian' attacks that had devastated so much of the Continent. Their remote geographical position had protected the Irish from the assaults of the Goths and Vandals, Magyars and Arabs; but the longships of the Norsemen, or Vikings, descended with the same terrible force on Ireland as they did on the coasts and rivers of Britain and Europe. The monasteries, filled with liturgical treasures, were a prime target for fierce pagan marauders, and suffered cruelly.

From 795 the Norsemen raided the coast of Ireland, growing progressively bolder with each attack. Finding rich pickings in the interior, they established themselves on the east coast and from time to time attempted full-scale invasions of the island. But ultimately they failed to extend their power beyond the ports they founded at Dublin, Waterford, Wexford and Limerick; these in the end constituted the most important Norse contribution to Irish history. Settling down, the Norsemen, now known as Ostmen, were absorbed into the shifting alliances of their Irish neighbours and even quarrelled among themselves. In the-

VIKING RULE IN IRELAND FINDS MATERIAL EXPRESSION IN THIS SILVER PENNY, MINTED IN DUBLIN AND PORTRAYING SHITRIC III (989-1029). TRADERS AS WELL AS WARRIORS, THE VIKINGS OR NORSEMEN OPENED IRELAND TO THE WIDER WORLD BY FOUNDING ITS FIRST REAL TOWNS, INCLUDING DUBLIN

VIKING LOOT, IN THE FORM OF AN 8TH- OR 9TH-CENTURY DOOR-RING FOUND IN A NORWEGIAN GRAVE-MOUND. IT IS CERTAINLY IRISH, AND WAS PROBABLY TAKEN FROM THE DOOR OF A MONASTERY. IN SCANDINAVIA A GOOD MANY IRISH-MADE OBJECTS HAVE BEEN DISCOVERED; SOME MAY HAVE REACHED THERE THROUGH TRADE, BUT ITEMS SUCH AS THIS ONE ARE LIKELY TO HAVE HAD A MORE VIOLENT HISTORY. SOME MONASTERIES WERE RANSACKED AGAIN AND AGAIN, BY NATIVE MARAUDERS AS WELL AS BY VIKINGS

SYMBOL OF FAITH. The Cross of Cong is one of the true masterpieces of medieval Irish art, elaborately worked in copper, silver and gold by an otherwise unknown craftsman named Maelisu. The Cross holds what was believed to be a fragment of the True Cross, while the crystal in the very centre of the cross probably housed the relic

late 10th century they were compelled to acknowledge the rising power of Munster, whose rulers had taken over the high kingship. Finally, in 1012, when the Norsemen and their allies revolted, they were defeated at Clontarf by High King Brian Boru and their political power was broken.

Brian Boru might perhaps have united the Irish, but he and his immediate heirs fell at Clontarf. Ireland remained divided and potentially vulnerable. Meanwhile, most of Britain had been conquered by the Anglo-Saxons and then, in 1066, by the Normans. Scotland and Wales remained Celtic societies, more or less akin to Ireland's, but England was ruled by a French-speaking elite with formidable military means: the armoured and mounted knight and the strong, safe castle.

The next great turning-point in Irish history came about in a classic 'Trojan Horse' episode. In 1166 Dermot MacMurrough, ejected from his kingdom of Leinster, fled to England and recruited a group of ambitious Normans to help him recover it. Pitted against foes with less sophisticated weaponry and tactical skills, Norman arms proved irresistible, and Dermot rewarded his allies lavishly. The most powerful and dangerous of them was Richard de Clare, Earl of Pembroke, nick-named Strongbow; he received the hand of Dermot's daughter, Aoife, and the succession to Dermot's kingdom. When Dermot died, Strongbow crushed a native revolt with Norman efficiency and made himself master of Leinster.

Strongbow's kingdom was short-lived. In 1171, unwilling to tolerate independent Norman lords on his flank, Henry II of England landed near Waterford with a papal blessing and a large army. He met with no resistance, and received the submission of both Normans and Irish as 'Lord of Ireland'.

MEDIEVAL IRELAND

AS LORD OF IRELAND, HENRY II RECOGNIZED STRONG-
BOW AS EARL OF LEINSTER, BUT CREATED A COUNTER-
WEIGHT TO STRONGBOW'S POWER BY NAMING ONE OF
HIS OWN MEN, HUGH DE LACY, AS THE EARL OF MEATH.

Other Anglo-Norman adventurers found a place within the new feudal arrangements, but Henry kept control of the ports in his own hands.
So began an ambiguous relationship between the English Crown and
the colonists, who alternated between claiming royal protection and
attempting to act independently – an alternation that would recur, in
various forms, for much of Ireland's history.

Over the following century or so, Anglo-Norman barons expanded
their holdings at the expense of the native
Irish, backed by superior military technology
and large numbers of land-hungry colonists
from England. Meanwhile, royal administrators tried to limit the barons' feudal privileges
and impose English-style institutions in Anglo-
Norman areas. An Irish parliament was set up,
the land was divided into counties, and the

RICHARD II'S FLEET DEPARTS FROM IRELAND
FOLLOWING HIS EXPEDITION OF 1399; ITS HISTORY
SHOWS THE DIFFICULTY OF MAINTAINING ENGLISH
RULE DURING THE MIDDLE AGES. RICHARD WAS
FORCED TO ABANDON HIS OPERATIONS BECAUSE
THE EXILED HENRY OF LANCASTER HAD LANDED
IN ENGLAND

legal system and the Church were remodelled.

By 1300 the Anglo-Normans controlled most of Ireland except Ulster and the far west. But then their fortunes changed for the worse. The grim struggle between the English and the Scots had a side effect in Ireland when Edward Bruce, brother of the Scottish king Robert Bruce, landed and attempted to make himself king. He was finally defeated and killed in 1318, but by the 1330s there were new upheavals. No longer at a military disadvantage, the native Irish began to regain territory. Colonization went into reverse as the effects of economic decline and a terrible plague, the Black Death, were felt. While the native Irish continued to make gains, intermarriage between the Anglo-Normans and the Irish was said to be making the newcomers 'more Irish than the Irish'. Rightly or wrongly, the Irish Parliament was alarmed enough to counter-attack with the Statutes of Kilkenny (1366), which prohibited colonists from inter-marrying with the native Irish or learning their language.

REGINALD'S TOWER, on the quayside at Waterford. The imposing 'drum' tower dates from approximately the 12th or 13th century and was reputedly the place where the Norman conquistador Strongbow married Dermot's daughter Aoife and established his claim to the throne of Leinster

Attempts were made to reassert royal control, notably by Richard II in the 1390s. But military expeditions achieved little, and other measures proved impossibly expensive. In the 15th century, weakened by foreign wars and internal problems, royal authority was effectively confined to a small area on the eastern seaboard around Dublin. Its defensive stance was empha-sized by the building of a rampart all the way round it. The rampart, or Pale, gave its name to the area under royal control; and the catch-phrase 'beyond the Pale' (uncivilized) neatly encapsulated the longstanding English attitude towards the Irish.

By the late 15th century it was clear that only the great Anglo-Norman magnates – the earls of Ormonde, Desmond and Kildare – were capable of maintaining any sort of order in the king's name, basing their power on wide lands and networks of family connections and alliances; by giving them a free rein, the Crown at least received a nominal allegiance. When the Earl of Kildare became the dominant magnate he was appointed Lord Deputy and, even though he had backed the losing Yorkist side in the Wars of the Roses, the victorious Tudor dynasty found it could not do without him.

AN UNCONQUERED KING. THE WEATHER-BEATEN STONE EFFIGY OF THE 13TH-CENTURY KING CONOR O'BRIEN LIES AMONG THE TRANQUIL RUINS OF CONCOMROE ABBEY IN COUNTY CLARE. THE O'BRIENS WERE NATIVE IRISH CHEIFS WHO SUCCESSFULLY RESISTED THE NORMAN NEWCOMERS

TUDOR CONQUEST

IN 1485, VICTORIOUS AT THE BATTLE OF BOSWORTH, HENRY TUDOR MADE GOOD HIS CLAIM TO THE ENGLISH THRONE AND WAS PROCLAIMED AS HENRY VII. HE AND HIS SUCCESSORS CREATED A NEW KIND OF STATE THAT WAS, BY THE STANDARDS OF THE TIME, UNPRECEDENTEDLY CENTRALIZED AND POWERFUL.

KING OF IRELAND. THE ENGLISH KING HENRY VIII (1509-47), PORTRAYED BY HANS HOLBEIN THE YOUNGER. HENRY'S BREAK WITH THE PAPACY AND HIS DISSOLUTION OF THE MONASTERIES WERE TO HAVE SERIOUS CONSEQUENCES FOR IRELAND, WHERE THE MAJORITY OF THE POPULATION HELD ONTO THEIR BELIEFS AND REMAINED TRUE TO THE OLD FAITH

Among the consequences was the first thoroughgoing English conquest of Ireland – and a religious divide that would bedevil relations between the two countries for centuries to come. The Tudors' success was not achieved rapidly. When Kildare continued to patronize Yorkist pretenders, Henry VII replaced him as Lord Deputy with Sir Edward Poynings. In 1494 the energetic new viceroy held a parliament at Drogheda which passed 'Poyning's Law', making it impossible for future Irish parliaments to meet or legislate without royal approval. Nevertheless Ireland remained too difficult – and too expensive – to govern while Kildare's supporters made trouble, and only two years later Henry felt obliged to restore the earl to office.

The Kildare earls retained their power into the 1530s, when they were overthrown and treated with unexpected severity by Henry VIII. Autocratic by temperament, Henry may also have been reacting to the Kildare faction's charges that he was a heretic, made at a time when he was repudiating the pope's authority and making himself the head of the English Church. Soon afterwards the Irish Parliament accepted Henry's 'Reformation' and recognized him as King (rather than the vaguer 'Lord') of Ireland. Henry's reign also marked the beginning of a 'surrender and regrant' policy, by which Gaelic lords who submitted to the king were confirmed in their lands, given English titles and expected to lead peaceful 'English' lives.

Under the last of the Tudors, Queen Elizabeth I (1558-1603), Protestantism became firmly established in England and was adopted as the state religion. By contrast, the great majority in Ireland remained faithful to Catholicism. This included both the Gaelic Irish and the 'Old English' descendants of the Anglo-Norman and other colonists; in time, despite the persistence of loyalty to the Crown among the Old English, the shared religion and shared misfortunes of the two groups would erase their differences.

Religion was not the only cause of conflict. Tudor efforts to impose English laws and customs sparked more than one Irish revolt, answered in turn by sporadic attempts to establish 'plantations' of loyal English settlers in various parts of the country. But matters grew serious as religious issues became increasingly more important, and Ireland was revealed as a security risk in 1580, when Italian and Spanish troops arrived to back the revolt of the Earl of Desmond.

The revolt was put down, but an even greater challenge was to arise in 1594. Hugh O'Neill, the chief of Gaelic Ulster, launched a carefully prepared rebellion that was widely supported. The degree of danger present elicited a commensurate response, leading to the defeat of O'Neill and his Spanish allies, and a determined reduction of his Ulster strongholds which ultimately completed the Elizabethan subjugation of Ireland.

THE ENGLISH ADVANCE. THE DISCIPLINE AND SUPERIOR EQUIPMENT OF ENGLISH TROOPS USUALLY GAVE THEM VICTORY IN OPEN BATTLE WITH THE IRISH. BUT WHEN THE IRISH TURNED TO GUERRILLA WARFARE, THEY WERE SUBDUED ONLY AFTER A HUGE INVESTMENT OF ENGLISH RESOURCES

THE SAVAGE CENTURY

WHEN HUGH O'NEILL SURRENDERED IN 1603, QUEEN ELIZABETH HAD ALREADY BEEN DEAD FOR THREE DAYS AND THE TUDOR DYNASTY HAD GIVEN WAY TO THE STUARTS. ELIZABETH WAS SUCCEEDED BY JAMES VI OF SCOTLAND, WHO NOW ALSO BECAME JAMES I OF ENGLAND.

The Stuart century was to be a savage and confused affair, in which king and parliament came into a fatal conflict, Scots and English waged war on each other, and events in Ireland, seemingly peripheral, had a marked influence on the destinies of all three kingdoms.

The first important development was 'the flight of the earls'. After their surrender, O'Neill and his ally, the Earl of Tyrconnell, had not been dispossessed; but in 1607, fearing arrest, they fled with their followers to the Continent. The government's response to the departure of the traditional leaders was a new and rigorous policy: the plantation of Ulster with English and Scots Protestants. Catholics

AT THE BATTLE OF THE BOYNE, fought on 1 July 1690. King William's army forced its way across the river and James II's troops withdrew. The Boyne became a great symbolic victory, but arguably James's failure of nerve (he fled from Ireland after the battle) doomed his cause. Even after this the Williamite victory was not easily won, and the Jacobites only laid down their arms, on honourable terms, in October 1691

The *Irish* Rebellion.

One hundred drown'd in a River.

THIS WOODCUT ILLUSTRATION FROM A CONTEMPORARY PAMPHLET CONDEMNS THE 1641 IRISH REBELLION, PICTURING IT AS A SERIES OF 'HORRIBLE MURDERS, PRODIGIOUS CRUELTIES, BARBAROUS VILLAINIES AND INHUMAN PRACTICES'

were not eliminated from Ulster, but the newcomers received most of the high-quality land, and what had been the most recalcitrantly Gaelic of the provinces became a Protestant stronghold.

In 1641 discontent among the Ulster Catholics flared up into a revolt that quickly spread to the rest of Ireland. Protestants were killed or driven from their homes, and in England rumours created a belief that there had been wholesale massacres in which tens of thousands perished. The immediate effect of the Irish revolt was to complicate the already difficult relations between King Charles I and Parliament, arguably to the point of making the English Civil War inevitable. The outbreak of the Civil War in 1642 gave the Irish rebels a breathing space but, even at this late date, divisions persisted between the Old English and the Gaelic Irish which prevented them from gaining control over the entire island. In 1649, after the English Civil War had ended in the triumph of Parliament and the execution of Charles I, Oliver Cromwell landed in Ireland with an army bent on avenging the 'massacres' of 1641.

Cromwell's swift, ruthless campaign included the notorious massacres that followed the capture of Wexford and Drogheda. But even more momentous in the long run was the land settlement that followed in 1653, once Cromwell's lieutenants had finished mopping-up operations. 'Disloyal' Catholic landowners were ejected in favour of English entrepreneurs, the only compensation being any properties they could secure for themselves beyond the Shannon, in Connaught; their choice was memorably summed up as 'Hell or Connaught!'

In this way the property-owning class in Ireland became overwhelmingly Protestant, while the peasantry remained Catholic. Some injustices were put right after the Restoration of Charles II in 1660, but the fundamental situation was unchanged. The advent of a Catholic king, James II (1685-88), briefly transformed the situation in Ireland, promising an early end to Protestant oppression. But the king rapidly alienated his English subjects and fled into exile; his throne was occupied by his Protestant daughter Mary and her Dutch husband William of Orange. (Hence Irish Protestants became 'Orangemen'.) With French help, James managed to land in Ireland, where the Catholic majority rallied to him.

The Irish on both sides fought well, but it was undoubtedly the new king, William III – William of Orange – who emerged victorious. Irish Protestant morale – and Protestant mythology – gained enormously from episodes such as their successful defence of Londonderry against James, and King William's subsequent victory in 1690 at the battle of the Boyne.

THE ASCENDANCY

RESISTANCE TO WILLIAM III'S FORCES ENDED IN OCTO-
BER 1691, WHEN THE DEFENDERS OF LIMERICK SIGNED A
TREATY WHICH ALLOWED SOLDIERS OF THE DEFEATED
ARMY TO LEAVE IRELAND.

These formed the first substantial contingent of the 'Wild Geese',
emigrants who took service abroad – mainly in the French army – and
made up Irish regiments that often saw action against their old enemy.

The other provision of the treaty was for a reasonably tolerant policy
towards the Catholic population. But whatever the intentions of the
government at Westminster, the Irish Parliament, now entirely Protes-
tant-dominated, was set on exploiting the Williamite victory to
the full. A series of penal laws deprived Catholics of their
remaining political rights and sought to prevent them from
ever increasing their small share in the ownership of the
land. Public life was now dominated by propertied
members of the episcopalian Church of Ireland (equivalent to the Anglican Church across the water); not
only the Catholic majority but the Dissenters – mainly
Presbyterians, numerous in the North – were shut out.
This situation, and the group that benefited from it,
became known as the Ascendancy.

The 18th century was the golden age of the Ascendancy. As in Britain, polished manners and the building
of fine town and country houses gave glamour to the lives
of a fortunate minority. Gifted Irishmen such as Oliver Goldsmith, Edmund Burke and R.B.Sheridan made their mark
in London, but public life in Dublin also
attracted talented men, notably Henry Grattan. As secure as they would ever be, the
Ascendancy leaders agitated against the government at Westminster, resenting the sub-
ordinate status of the Irish Parliament and the
English laws that discriminated against Irish
products. Their objections to Ireland's colonial
status became more forceful with the success of the American colonists
in overthrowing George III's 'tyranny', and Grattan's campaign reached
a climax in 1782 when the Irish parliament was recognized as a separate
and independent institution under the Crown.

In practice, British influence remained paramount, exercised through
the viceroy – the Lord Lieutenant – and a network of patronage and
bribery. Further reforms would have been possible only with Catholic
support. But although many Catholic disabilities were removed in the
1790s, Ascendancy leaders clung to their own monopolies – the right to
be an MP and to hold government office. The situation was complicated
by the spread of radical ideas in the wake of the 1789 French Revolution.

REBEL HERO. WOLFE TONE (1763-98) WAS
ONE OF THE FOUNDERS OF THE REPUBLICAN SOCIETY
OF UNITED IRISHMEN, INSPIRED BY THE FRENCH
REVOLUTION. CAPTURED WHILE ATTEMPTING TO
BRING FRENCH HELP TO THE 1798 RISING, HE WAS
SENTENCED TO HANG BUT COMMITTED SUICIDE

By the 1790s Britain was at war with France and harshly suppressing any sign of dissent at home. In 1798, the radical, non-sectarian Society of United Irishmen attempted a rising, but although both Ulster Presbyterians and southern Catholics were among the rebels, ominous and violent signs of religious antagonism began to appear. In the event, the rising was brutally put down and its best-known leaders, Lord Edward Fitzgerald and Wolfe Tone, perished.

AUGUSTAN ASSEMBLY. FRANCIS WHEATLEY'S GROUP PORTRAIT OF THE IRISH HOUSE OF COMMONS CAPTURES THE SUPREME CONFIDENCE OF THE 18TH-CENTURY UPPER CLASS. WHEN IT WAS PAINTED IN 1780, THE ASSEMBLED LEGISLATORS CAN HARDLY HAVE ANTICIPATED THAT TWENTY YEARS LATER MANY OF THEM WOULD VOTE TO END THEIR COLLECTIVE EXISTENCE

THE GREAT HUNGER

AFTER THE 1798 REVOLT, PITT'S GOVERNMENT DECIDED ON A DRAMATIC CHANGE OF POLICY. JUST AS IN 1707, WHEN ENGLAND AND SCOTLAND HAD BEEN UNITED, IRELAND AND GREAT BRITAIN WERE TO BE JOINED BY AN ACT OF UNION.

Instead of being a separate country under the British Crown – with, in practice, a colonial status – Ireland would be part of an enlarged British state with a new name: the United Kingdom.

Ireland's Parliament would cease to exist, but Irish constituencies would elect MPs to serve at Westminster. The proposal needed the consent of the Irish Parliament, which was all too accustomed to a politics based on the distribution of favours; and after some bribery and horse-trading on a larger-than-usual scale the Act of Union was passed in June 1800 and took effect in 1801.

Most members of the Ascendancy adapted to the situation, and the only violent reaction was an ineffectual rising by the United Irishmen in 1803 which merely added the name of its leader, Robert Emmet, to the pantheon of Irish martyrs. A positive way of exploiting the new situation was devised by a brilliant lawyer named Daniel O'Connell. He created an organization that made Catholics a political force, and used mass-meetings and other forms of peaceful, legal agitation to further his twin aims of Catholic Emancipation and repeal of the Union.

EMMET STANDS TRIAL. IN 1803, WHEN THE YOUNG ROBERT EMMET (1778-1803) ATTEMPTED TO RAISE DUBLIN AGAINST BRITISH RULE, THE RESULT WAS A FIASCO. EMMET WAS CONDEMNED TO DEATH, BUT HIS DEFIANT SPEECH BECAME AN INSPIRATION FOR FUTURE GENERATIONS OF IRISH PATRIOTS

Catholic emancipation had been on the British political agenda for a long time, having been implicitly promised as part of the campaign to bring about the Union; but it had foundered on the objections of King George III. The issue came to a head again in 1828, when O'Connell was elected as MP for Clare but, as a Catholic, was unable to take his seat. The government was finally convinced that religious discrimination had to end, and new legislation made it possible at last for both Catholics and Dissenters to become MPs and hold office under the Crown.

O'Connell was less successful in agitating for the repeal of the Union, and there were signs that a new generation might repudiate his strictly constitutional politics. But the entire situation was transformed when Ireland was devastated by the Great Famine of 1845-50. Early 19th-century Ireland was a miserably poor country in which the economic advances of the previous century had been wiped out by British competition and galloping population growth. By the mid-1840s there were twice as many Irish – over eight million – as there had been fifty years earlier. Subsisting on tiny holdings and dependent on a single crop, the potato, the peasant masses were helpless when a blight appeared in 1845 and destroyed the entire harvest the following year. The crisis was mishandled by British governments which vacillated between supplying relief and relying on sluggish market forces. In scenes of horror and squalor, almost a million people perished and another million emigrated, many of them forming the nucleus of a bitterly anti-British community in the United States.

THE FAMINE is one of the cardinal facts of Irish history, still vivid in the popular memory. Ireland's peasant millions were dependent on a single crop, the potato, and the harvest failures from 1845 onwards left them helpless. As in so many crises, government responses were slow and ill-conceived

DUBLIN HAILS 'THE LIBERATOR', DANIEL O'CONNELL (1775-1847), NEWLY RELEASED FROM PRISON IN SEPTEMBER 1844. O'CONNELL'S CRIME WAS TO HAVE AGITATED PEACEFULLY AND LEGALLY FOR THE REPEAL OF THE UNION AND IRISH SELF-GOVERNMENT. THE FAMINE WRECKED O'CONNELL'S CAMPAIGN, AND HE DIED IN 1847

THE HOME RULE ISSUE

THE CONSEQUENCES OF THE FAMINE WERE LONG-LAST-ING. IRELAND BECAME A COUNTRY THAT THE YOUNG, POOR AND HOPEFUL MADE HASTE TO LEAVE, ENCOURAGED BY FRIENDS AND RELATIVES WHO HAD ALREADY MADE MORE SECURE AND PROSPEROUS LIVES FOR THEMSELVES ABROAD.

The decline in Ireland's population went on and on, into the 20th century. Mass evictions during and after the Famine bred a hatred of the Ascendancy landlords, giving an economic dimension to the coming political struggles. And although a starving people scarcely stirred when called on to revolt in 1848, revolutionary sentiment revived with the founding of the Fenians, or Irish Republican Brotherhood, who attempted a rising in 1867.

This helped to convince the Liberal prime minister, Gladstone, that his mission was 'to pacify Ireland'. Moreover Irish politicians were beginning to have an impact at Westminster. Reform Acts had given many more people the right to vote – including many more Irish

PARNELL TRIUMPHANT, RE-ELECTED AS THE LEADER OF THE NATIONALIST PARTY IN THE BRITISH PARLIAMENT. BUT THIS MOST ICILY DETERMINED ADVOCATE OF HOME RULE WAS BROUGHT DOWN BY A POLITICALLY ENGINEERED DIVORCE SCANDAL

. When Home Rule for Ireland appeared to be politically feasible, opposition intensified in the Protestant areas of the North, led by the barrister-MP Sir Edward Carson (centre, with a stick). For a time, civil war seemed likely

people – and the introduction of the secret ballot in 1872 meant that tenants could no longer be intimidated by their landlords. As a result, in the 1870s a large group of Irish Nationalist MPs, committed to Home Rule (that is, self-government), appeared in the House of Commons; led by the coldly brilliant Charles Stewart Parnell, they were able to influence events by holding up the proceedings or political manoeuvring. The Nationalists were all the more effective because of their links with Michael Davitt's Land League, which was staging rent strikes and boycotts to assert the rights of tenant farmers. Parnell's tortuous relationship with Gladstone encouraged 'the Old Man' to remedy a number of Irish grievances. Eventually Gladstone was converted to Home Rule, but his attempts to pass it into law led to a split in his own party and foundered on the opposition of the House of Lords. A divorce scandal ruined Parnell, leaving the Nationalists in confusion, and the retirement of Gladstone was swiftly followed by a series of Conservative administrations committed to the Union. Their policy, 'killing Home Rule with kindness', effected a quiet social revolution in Ireland by issuing credits that enabled tenants to buy the land they worked from their landlords.

Home Rule became a live issue again after the great Liberal victory of 1906. A constitutional crisis in 1909-11 led to the abolition of the House of Lords' absolute veto, making it possible for the Liberal-Nationalist majority in the House of Commons to secure Home Rule. But Protestant hostility had been growing towards the prospect of living in a country with a Catholic majority, and there was a particularly unbending mood in the concentrated Protestant communities in Ulster. Fighting talk by the Ulster leader, Edward Carson, was encouraged by the Conservative Opposition, and arms were illicitly run in for volunteer militias of both persuasions that formed in the North and Dublin. A hostile declaration by British officers at the Curragh raised the possibility that the army would refuse to obey the government. In this tense situation, with Home Rule passed and some kind of opt-out for Ulster under consideration, the First World War broke out and the entire problem was shelved.

THE CALL TO ARMS, 1914. The outbreak of the First World War led to a British recruitment drive in Ireland. The poster deploys traditional symbols, exploiting Irish fellow-feeling for 'little Belgium', a country brutally violated by imperial Germany. Many Irishmen did volunteer and died in bloody battle

THE EASTER RISING

MANY IRISH NATIONALISTS BACKED THE CAMPAIGN FOR HOME RULE CONDUCTED BY THE PARLIAMENTARY PARTY. BUT GROUPS SUCH AS THE IRISH REPUBLICAN BROTHER-HOOD REMAINED FAITHFUL TO THE REVOLUTIONARY AND SEPARATIST TRADITION.

The inconclusive turn of events in 1914 increased their distrust of British intentions. The schoolteacher-poet Patrick Pearse and other members of the Brotherhood planned to lead the Irish Volunteers, a nationalist self-defence force, in a revolt against British rule, helped by the Irish Citizen Army, a trade union and socialist force led by James Connolly.

On the outbreak of war many Irishmen had joined the British army to fight in France, and even in 1916 the general mood in Ireland was far from revolutionary. Divisions of opinion within the Volunteers led to a confused sequence of orders and cancellations, so that many Volunteers failed to turn out on Easter Monday, 24 April 1916. In all of Ireland only a few thousand men – less than two thousand in Dublin – were involved in what became the epic Easter Rising. At noon on the Monday, a few dozen men with rifles marched down Sackville Street (present-day O'Connell Street) and proceeded to take possession of the General Post Office, a solid, spacious classical building in the heart of Dublin. Shortly afterwards, Pearse went outside and proclaimed the setting up of a Provisional Government of the Irish Republic. The GPO was fortified, barricades sealed off the streets, and snipers moved out on to the roofs. Elsewhere in the city, small contingents took up positions in the Four Courts and other places, ready to oppose any British advance.

Failing to realize how small the rebel numbers were, the British authorities reacted cautiously, drafting in troops from other parts of Ireland. Barricades were smashed by artillery fire, and Sackville Street was shelled – by, among other things, a gunboat on the river Liffey. The insurgents resisted with remarkable determination, even when it was clear that there had been no general rising and hopes of German help had faded. On the fifth day, fires started by incendiary bombs drove the rebels from the GPO. They took refuge in a row of houses nearby but, with the end in

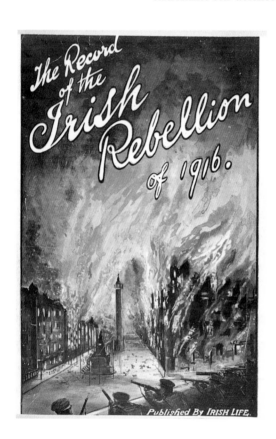

A HEROIC ENTERPRISE. ON THE COVER OF THIS MAGAZINE SPECIAL ISSUE, THE EASTER RISING IS ALREADY BEING PORTRAYED AS AN APOCALYPTIC EVENT. BARRICADES WERE SMASHED BY ARYILLERY FIRE, AND SACKVILLE STREET WAS SHELLED. THE HANDFUL OF MEN WHO SEIZED DUBLIN'S GENERAL POST OFFICE CHANGED HISTORY BY BECOMING MARTYRS TO A REVIVED REPUBLICAN CAUSE

sight and civilian lives in danger, Pearse authorized an unconditional surrender.

Dubliners showed little sympathy when the prisoners were marched away, and some flung rotten fruit at them. But Irish opinion changed rapidly when Pearse, Connolly and thirteen others were court-martialled and shot; Connolly, badly wounded, was executed strapped to a chair. Later Sir Roger Casement, a former colonial official who had been captured after landing in Ireland from a German U-boat, was tried and hanged. To the British the dead men were traitors; to the Irish they became martyrs.

Other developments, including a mishandled effort to impose conscription on Ireland, swelled the rising tide of republicanism. At the first post-war election, in December 1918, the hitherto dominant Nationalist Party was swept away and, everywhere outside the North, the victor was a militantly republican party, Sinn Fein ('Ourselves Alone'). Its representatives refused to take their seats at Westminster, setting up their own assembly and administration in Dublin in defiance of the British government. The stage was set for another confrontation.

DUBLIN BLITZED. The damage done by the British bombardment of rebel positions in Dublin is vividly conveyed by this photograph of gutted houses on Eden Quay and Sackville Street, taken from the Carlisle Bridge; the rebel headquarters, the General Post Office, is just outside the picture. The British over-reaction was perhaps understandable in the middle of a World War, but the subsequent executions of rebel leaders proved to be fatal misjudgements, permanently alienating most Irish opinion

SIR ROGER CASEMENT WAS A FORMER BRITISH COLONIAL OFFICIAL, ADMIRED FOR HIS HUMANITARIAN WORK IN AFRICA. DURING WORLD WAR I, HE FAILED TO OBTAIN GERMAN HELP FOR AN IRISH REBELLION AND RETURNED, HOPING TO PREVENT A FUTILE RISING. MOST OF THE REBEL LEADERS WERE SHOT, BUT CASEMENT WAS TRIED AS A TRAITOR AND HANGED

TWO IRELANDS

THE STAND-OFF BETWEEN SINN FEIN AND THE BRITISH AUTHORITIES SOON LED TO FIGHTING. THE GUERRILLA CAMPAIGN WAGED BY SINN FEIN'S MILITARY WING, THE IRISH REPUBLICAN ARMY (IRA), LED TO AN EVER MORE VICIOUS ROUND OF ATROCITIES AND REPRISALS COMMITTED BY BOTH SIDES.

The IRA waged a ruthless campaign, but it was British-employed irregulars, nicknamed 'the Black and Tans', who became particularly notorious for uncontrolled violence. After almost three years of conflict and turbulence (1919-21), both sides recognized that the IRA could neither be defeated nor win an outright victory. The treaty signed in December 1921 partitioned Ireland. Six counties in the North remained within the United Kingdom; the other twenty-six counties became the Irish Free State, a self-governing dominion that continued to owe allegiance to the Crown.

The republican representatives, including the IRA leader Michael Collins, had signed reluctantly, believing that they had no option. They were denounced as traitors by one wing of the movement, led by Eamon de Valera. The rejectionists lost the elections that followed, but continuing conflicts escalated into a civil war every bit as bloody and uncompromising as the fight against the British; among the casualties was Michael Collins, who was assassinated. The government forces won, but for some years bitter feelings persisted and sporadic acts of violence occurred.

Even the leaders of Northern Ireland did not expect Partition to be permanent; but the new arrangements proved surprisingly durable. The North was part of the United Kingdom, but in practice it was left to run its own affairs through its parliament at Stormont. Although it had a substantial Catholic and Nationalist minority, Northern Ireland was dominated by Protestant Unionists, not only politically but also in terms of social and economic privileges.

Unlike the Free State, it was an industrialized area, well known for linen manufactures and shipbuilding. Its standard of living was much higher than that of the South, although its economy was vulnerable and the Great Depression of the 1930s brought appallingly high unemployment.

MICHAEL COLLINS (1890-1922) PERSONIFIED THE TRAGIC DIVISIONS WITHIN IRISH NATIONALISM. A MILITARY AND POLITICAL LEADER IN THE STRUGGLE AGAINST BRITISH RULE, HE RELUCTANTLY SIGNED THE TREATY THAT PARTITIONED IRELAND. TEN DAYS AFTER BECOMING HEAD OF THE PROVISIONAL GOVERNMENT, HE WAS AMBUSHED AND KILLED BY ANTI-PARTITIONISTS

THE GREAT SURVIVOR. Eamon de Valera (1882-1975) addresses a crowd at Cork in 1922. 'Dev' was a rebel commander during the Easter Rising, but escaped execution because he held an American passport. In 1922 he opposed the Anglo-Irish treaty, but he ultimately re-entered politics as leader of the newly-founded Fianna Fail party. Several times prime minister, he dominated Irish politics until his retirement in 1959

Meanwhile the Free State was evolving into a very different society. Led by De Valera from 1932, it progressively loosened its ties with the United Kingdom. In 1937, having acquired a new constitution, Eire (as the country was now generally known) became a republic in all but name; it also gave a special status to the Catholic Church as 'Guardian of the Faith'. Eire remained neutral during the Second World War, when, by contrast, Belfast was heavily bombed. In 1949 it formally became a republic, further distancing itself from Britain by leaving the Commonwealth. For several decades the position remained substantially unchanged. Unionism reigned in the North,

where the Nationalists remained quiescent and sporadic action by militants using the old IRA name achieved little. De Valera's vision of a rural, pious Ireland seemed realized in the South, but emigrants continued to vote with their feet against its economic backwardness. Things began to change after de Valera's retirement as Taoiseach (prime minister) in 1959, and for both Irelands the 1960s would prove to be a watershed.

LIFE DOWN THE AGES

LEFT: Life in the country: carrying home the turf
RIGHT: Connemara Mountains, County Galway

LIFE IN THE COUNTRY: A small farm in the Mourne Mountains

HISTORY HAS NOT BEEN PARTICULARLY KIND
TO IRELAND, BUT IN EVERY GENERATION
THE IRISH HAVE NURTURED THEIR SPECIAL
QUALITIES AND MAINTAINED THEIR OWN
DISTICTIVE WAY OF LIFE

43

HUNTERS AND FARMERS

WE HAVE SOME EVIDENCE ABOUT HOW THE FIRST IN-
HABITANTS OF IRELAND LIVED, THOUGH WE ARE NEVER
LIKELY TO KNOW VERY MUCH ABOUT THEIR THOUGHTS
AND FEELINGS.

The families that crossed the Irish Sea from Scotland were in the
Mesolithic (Middle Stone Age) phase of development. That is, their
stone tools and weapons were relatively advanced, but they were still
hunter-gatherers, living on what they could catch or pick. Their way of

MYSTERIOUS STONE CIRCLES are found in large
numbers, especially in the south-west of Ireland; this one
is Drombeg Circle in County Clare. They are presumed
to have been meeting places for religious rituals, perhaps
built on the basis of astronomical observations

life kept them on the move, but traces of
dwellings made of wattle (branches) have been
found at Mount Sandel, County Londonderry,
which show that at times they were able to settle and subsist on a diet of fishes, birds, berries
and nuts. Sites have also been identified where
they manufactured arrows, spears and hand-axes.

Much more is known about the Irish of the Neolithic (New Stone
Age), who farmed the land, domesticated cattle, sheep and goats, wove
textiles and made pottery. Excavations at Ballynagilly, in County Tyrone,
have uncovered evidence of a square house, made from planks of oak,
which dates back to about 3200 BC. But the most exciting find so far,
dating from about the same time, was made under two metres of blanket
bog at the Ceide Fields in County Mayo: the remains of an entire community, including a network of drystone-walled enclosures.

If this suggests that Neolithic society was well-organized and capable

of co-operative effort, the thousand or more megalithic tombs scattered all over Ireland leave no room for doubt. The three main types are court tombs, portal tombs or dolmens, and passage graves. All involved one or more interments within a burial chamber that consisted of a stone structure covered by a mound. Many have been stripped of their earth covering in the course of the millennia, so that they, and especially the dolmens ('stone tables'), now rise up from the landscape in a dramatically sculpturesque fashion. However, in scale there is nothing to match the great mound-covered passage tombs, with their stone-lined interiors and geometric ornamentation; the largest of all, the Newgrange tumulus, is an awe-inspiring sight, 13 metres high and 80 metres across.

Since the tombs contained many remains and seem to have been used over a number of generations, this was evidently a stable society as well as a formidably organized one. The presence of grave goods makes it almost certain that the tombs were not just memorials, but embodied beliefs about some kind of life after death.

Equally significant ideas must have driven on the Bronze Age Irish who constructed wedge tombs, stone circles and standing stones. They were also miners, finding gold as well as the copper used to make bronze weapons and ornaments. The tin needed to turn copper into bronze had to be imported, but Irish mines were so rich, and Irish craftsmen so skillful, that Irish exports found their way all over Europe.

MIGHTY TOMB. ABOUT 13 METRES HIGH AND 80 METRES ACROSS, NEWGRANGE IS THE MOST CELEBRATED OF ALL IRELAND'S NEOLITHIC PASSAGE TOMBS. SOME OF THE MATERIALS USED WERE BROUGHT FROM CONSIDERABLE DISTANCES. THE GLEAMING WHITE QUARTZITE THAT LINES THE OUTSIDE IS A CONTROVERSIAL MODERN RECONSTRUCTION

THE CELTIC WORLD

SOMEWHERE AROUND 350 BC, IRELAND ENTERED THE
IRON AGE AND THEN, IF NOT EARLIER, BECAME A CELTIC,
GAELIC-SPEAKING SOCIETY.

Scholars are now more reluctant than they were in the past to describe cultural changes in terms of invasions by new peoples, but it does seem likely that invader-settlers played a large part in the Celticization of Ireland; one strong piece of evidence is the existence in Irish Gaelic of words that can only be pre-Celtic, implying that the dominant Gaels had at some point absorbed an earlier group or groups.

The Celts of Ireland were effectively illiterate until the establishment of Christianity. As a consequence, what we know about Celtic society is based on archaeological evidence, Roman observations of the Celts (almost everywhere except in Ireland), and the work of monastic scribes, who recorded surviving oral traditions and the behaviour of their own still-Celtic contemporaries. Since the resulting picture makes no allowance for differences over place and time, it may be inaccurate in some details, but it is probably broadly true.

Celtic Ireland was certainly a land of many *tuatha*, or kingdoms. Based on kinship ties and a rigid social hierarchy, the *tuath* embodied the values of an aristocratic warrior caste. The king did not inherit his position, but was elected by an assembly of freemen from an élite family group. For most other purposes society was dominated by the aristocracy, whose members varied greatly in status and prestige. These were mainly determined by how many clients or dependents a noble possessed. The clients (roughly comparable to feudal vassals) were freemen who received the use of the lord's cattle in return for payments in kind and labour services. Although arable farming provided Ireland's staple foods, cattle conferred prestige, serving as an equivalent to money and the chief prize of war. Indeed, the unceasing wars of Celtic Ireland were arguably little more than tit-for-tat cattle raids, conducted as an aristocratic sport, which had little effect on the ordinary round of life.

Below the freemen were the unfree ('serfs'), as well as many slaves. Slavery continued for centuries into the Christian era. Concubinage, which the Church found more offensive, also proved hard to eradicate. According to the Celtic legal code, the Brehon Law, concubines had

THE TORC, OR NECK RING, WAS A DISTINCTIVELY CELTIC MEANS OF ADORNMENT OR CEREMONIAL DISPLAY. OFTEN FOUND IN PRINCELY BURIALS AND SEEN ON IMAGES OF THE CELTIC GODS, IT ALMOST CERTAINLY INDICATED THAT ITS MALE OR FEMALE OWNER WAS A PERSON OF HIGH STATUS. THIS 3RD CENTURY BC TORC, FOUND IN A BOG IN THE CLONMACNOISE AREA, IS MADE OF GOLD AND IS A FINE EXAMPLE OF ACCURATE CRAFTSMANSHIP

definite rights, becoming in effect supplementary wives when they bore children. The laws were complex enough to give employment to specialists, and the *breitheamh* (lawyer), like the *file* (bard) and the skilled craftsman, was a freeman with a rather distinct, privileged position that put him somewhat outside the main social structure. The bard and the craftsmen were privileged beings because their works – praise-poems and fine weapons and ornaments – were the very stuff on which the king's own renown depended.

Celtic Ireland was an essentially rural society, with no real towns and little trade until the arrival of the Viking invaders. Despite its imposing fortresses at Tara, Emain Macha and elsewhere, it was essentially a small-scale world, albeit one that became, in folk-memory, mighty and heroic.

SHIP OF GOLD. This delightful little object is part of a hoard of gold objects found at Broighter, County Londonderry, in 1896. Although it dates from the 1st century BC or the 1st century AD, its mast, benches and oars have all been preserved

ABBOTS, ACETICS AND SCRIBES

LIKE SO MANY THINGS IRISH, THE CAREERS OF MANY OF THE ISLAND'S EARLY CHURCHMEN INVOLVED A SERIES OF INTERESTING PARADOXES.

The boastful bardic warrior-society of the Celts, once it was committed to Christianity, brought forth solitaries who wished to pass their lives in humility and obscurity. But as word of their holiness spread, disciples

CLONMACNOISE, ONE OF THE CENTRES OF EARLY IRISH MONASTICISM, ON THE RIVER SHANNON. THIS VIEW OF ITS EXTENSIVE RUINS SHOWS A 9TH-CENTURY CELTIC CROSS AND THE ROOFLESS O'ROURKE'S TOWER

gathered round them and the anchorites were reluctantly transformed into the abbots or abbesses of famous monasteries, patronized by kings, supervising scribes and acquiring precious objects for increasingly splendid church services. As the Irish reputation for learning spread, students flocked in from Britain and the Continent, and the most celebrated monastic settlements became bustling communities, the nearest things to towns that could be found in pre-Viking Ireland.

Irish literature has left a number of pictures of early Christian life. Some emphasize heroic self-mortification, but others are more directly joyful, like this evocation of St Columba's experiences on Iona, with its unusual feeling for nature: 'I find it delightful to dwell on a little island, on the peak of a rock from which I can look out on the calm sea...its splendid flocks of birds over the swelling ocean. . . its mighty whales, greatest of wonders.' But then Columba took an equal delight in poring over books, kneeling in prayer, singing psalms, gathering seaweed, fishing and feeding the poor, before finally retiring to his cell.

Columba preserved a relative simplicity of life by remaining on Iona, sending out surplus disciples to evangelize Scotland. The restless activity that drove on Irish missionaries from place to place may perhaps have represented a comparable attempt to avoid settling down as the head of a community, involved with worldly affairs (though most of them came to it in the end). Not that the great Irish monasteries were necessarily corrupt. But they were very much of and in the world, and they were certainly different from monasteries elsewhere in Christendom. They were far more important than bishoprics; instead of belonging to monastic orders following a known 'rule', they were self-governing and self-defining; and as well as owning large estates, they were often caught up in tribal politics.

These and other peculiarities of the Celtic church were largely the result of the isolation in which it had developed, without any significant contact with Rome. When such contacts did begin to be made, initially when Celtic and papal-appointed missionaries met in Britain, it became apparent that the Irish were out of line in many respects, from their dating of Easter to the power exercised by layman-abbots. A drive for uniformity within the Irish Church reached its climax in the early 12th century, when St Malachy and others divided Ireland into dioceses run by bishops, deprived the monasteries of much of their land, and put them under the control of Cistercians and other foreign orders. Whatever their merits, the reforms did lead to the decay of the monastic schools, ending the cultural influence of the monasteries. The changes were in place before the Anglo-Norman invasion, but the newcomers would nevertheless represent their arrival as a triumph of civilization over barbarism, in religion as in other matters.

IRISH COSTUME of the 11th century is portrayed in these meditative and rather melancholy figures which are part of a group in high relief on the bronze cover of the Breac Maedhoc shrine, made for St Maedhoc of Drumlane. Realism is integrated with a form of wave-like patterning in a very impressive manner

A MEDIEVAL IRISH PRIEST BLOWS ST PATRICK'S HORN. THIS IS ONE OF MANY VIVID ILLUSTRATIONS IN A COPY (BODLEIAN LIBRARY, OXFORD) OF THE 12TH-CENTURY ACCOUNT OF IRELAND, PREJUDICED BUT INVALUABLE, WRITTEN BY GERALD OF WALES

WILD IRISH & CIVIL IRISH

THE EFFECT OF THE ANGLO-NORMAN INVASION AT THE
END OF THE 12TH CENTURY WAS TO DIVIDE IRELAND
BETWEEN THE NEWCOMERS (KNOWN AS THE 'OLD ENG-
LISH' EVEN CENTURIES AFTER THEY HAD SETTLED) AND
THE GAELIC-SPEAKING AND 'CELTIC' IRISH.

The *Topography of Ireland* by Gerald of Wales gives us a comprehen-
sive, if jaundiced, account of Irish society just after the Normans had
established themselves. Gerald was an Anglo-Norman cleric related to
the FitzGeralds, who were taking a prominent part in the conquest of
Ireland, and he visited the country several times. He clearly wished to
please his master, Henry II, by justifying the
invasion as a civilizing mission, but there is no
reason to suppose that he was not genuinely
shocked by the deviant aspects and apparent
laxness of the Irish Church, or by the barbarism of the Irish in general. Apart from
moral shortcomings in which they may or may
not have surpassed the Normans, the barbarism of the Irish mainly consisted in looking
and behaving differently from them. Instead of
cropped hair, neat beards and short cloaks, the
Irish sported flowing locks and beards. They
wore shirts and long mantles and – though
Gerald is a little vague on the subject – no
breeches, going barefoot and bare-legged.
Their horsemanship and their fighting meth-
ods were equally un-Norman.

AN IRISH KING AND HIS SUBJECTS, FEASTING
ON MARE'S FLESH DURING A CORONATION RITUAL;
FROM THE COPY OF GERALD OF WALES' ACCOUNT
OF IRELAND IN THE BODLEIAN LIBRARY, OXFORD.
AS THE ILLUSTRATION ON THE RIGHT DEMONSTRATES,
BRITISH ATTITUDES TOWARDS IRISH CUSTOMS
CHANGED REMARKABLY LITTLE OVER THE CENTURIES

Gerald was equally damning about Irish
'laziness' in failing to till the soil, describing a
pastoral society in which milk and butter were
all-purpose staple foods. He rather underestimated the importance of
grain-growing, but there is little doubt that the Normans did increase
production in the eastern areas where they were most firmly in control,
introducing the feudal system, parceling out the land into manors with
large open fields and rotating crops as they did in England. For a time
they were able to produce surpluses, trade in wool and grain, and main-
tain the prosperity of the Irish ports.

However, there were strict limits to their success, since yields were
low and the social and economic fabric was fragile. Wills and other docu-
ments reveal that the settlers had few household goods and clothes,
though they were better off in that respect than the native Irish. Later,
Bruce's invasion, the 14th-century recession and the Black Death had a
devastating effect. The Gaelic Irish, forced back into the woods, bogs
and other marginal lands, began to regain ground. The Old English,
feeling increasingly beleaguered, believed that many of their number

were becoming 'more Irish than the Irish' and made laws that were intended to stop them.

Most historians now think that Old English fears of cultural extinction were wildly exaggerated. Despite some assimilation, the two groups remained visibly different. By the 16th century the difference was being described and illustrated in terms of two native types: the 'Civil Irish', who lived in towns, dressed in buttoned-up Tudor fashion, and were obedient to the Crown; and the unkempt and still-barefoot 'Wild Irish'.

The contemporary improvement in Tudor living standards pointed up the difference. The

AN ALFRESCO FEAST. In this 16th-century woodcut, the chief of the MacSweynes is seated at dinner. Since the woodcut comes from an English book, it emphasizes the barbarity of the proceedings – the lack of a proper table, the proximity of the slaughtering and cooking, and the less than delicate manners of all concerned

Gaelic Irish did undoubtedly live in more primitive style, but it is also true that observers conveniently forgot what a difference a few years make: even as the English traveller noted with distaste that most of the Irish had no mattresses, old-fashioned moralists in his own country were lamenting the fact that the yeoman's log had been replaced by a new-fangled and doubtless decadent pillow.

WILD AND CIVIL IRISH AS PORTRAYED IN
NEAT LITTLE VIGNETTES BESIDE A MAP OF IRELAND
BY ONE HONDIUS JOCODUS, 1616. WILD OR CIVIL,
BARBAROUS OR CIVILIZED, THE CRITERION IS CLEAR:
PEOPLE WHO DO NOT FOLLOW JACOBEAN ENGLISH
STYLES IN APPEARANCE AND CLOTHING ARE OUTSIDE
THE CHARMED CIRCLE OF CIVILIZATION

For most of the medieval and early modern periods, descriptions of Irish life mainly reflect English values. A different point of view is expressed by a bardic tirade against those who cut their hair short and in other respects 'follow English ways'. Writing in the 16th century, Laoiseach Mac an Bhaird contrasts such effete Irishmen with one Eoghan the Fair-Haired, 'the darling of noble women' and 'a man who never loved English customs' – two characteristics that appear to have been closely related in the poet's mind. Eoghan would give his breeches away for a trifle, and he has no use for a cloak or doublet and hose, let alone a high-necked ruff. He would prefer to sleep on rushes rather than in a feather bed, and to live in a wattle house rather than a castle (hardly true of most Gaelic lords). Above all he relishes taking part in a fight, especially against the foreigner. Eoghan, says the poet approvingly, 'has chosen the wild life'.

Even if Laoiseach's exaltation of the wild, free life is in part an imaginative fantasy, its ideals are strikingly at odds with the Tudor vision of order. Long after the bardic tradition faded away, something of Laoiseach's admiration for wild ways survived in the Irish psyche, for example re-emerging in J. M. Synge's famous drama *The Playboy of the Western World*, in which the young fugitive Christy Mahon turns up at a Mayo village and, claiming to have killed his father with a single blow, finds himself greatly admired – most of all by the women and girls.

Nevertheless the future did not lie with free-living Eoghan, or with those who exalted him. The 17th century ruined the bards by destroying the social order which had sustained them. The Gaelic heartland of Ulster ceased to be 'wild' when colonized early in the century by Protestant settlers from England and Scotland. Then the wars of Cromwell and William of Orange effectively destroyed the Catholic landowning class in most of Ireland, creating a social hierarchy that was based on religion but expressed itself most directly in terms of class. In Ulster, Presbyterianism and other non-episcopalian forms of Protestantism had a large following; but almost everywhere else the ruling class belonged to the established Church of Ireland (equivalent to the Anglican Church), while the peasant masses adhered to Roman Catholicism.

William III's victory ended Catholic hopes of reversing the situation, and the era of the Protestant 'Ascendancy' began. Its members, English-speaking and belonging to the Church of Ireland, are commonly described as Anglo-Irish, although the term is misleading if it is taken to imply that they were somehow not really Irish. During the 18th century, thanks to their privileged position, the Anglo-Irish were the principal makers of Irish history, and even afterwards their contribution to the national life was quite remarkable.

A CIVILIZED ELEGANCE WAS ACHIEVED BY THE 18TH-CENTURY ANGLO-IRISH ELITE. HERE IS ONE OF MANY SUCH IMAGES, CAPTURED BY THE BRUSH OF AN IMPORTED ENGLISH ARTIST. FRANCIS WHEATLEY: THE EARL OF ANTRIM DRIVING A PHAETON IN GLENARM CASTLE PARK, BALLYMENA

THE IRISH AT WAR

CELTIC LEGEND EXALTS THE DOOMED WARRIOR-HERO WHO IS STRONG ENOUGH TO HOLD ENTIRE ARMIES AT BAY. THIS WAS NO DOUBT THE IDEAL OF THE ACTUAL CELTIC ARISTOCRACY, EMBODIED IN THEIR LARGE AND COMPLEX FORMIDABLE IRON SWORDS, LARGE AND COMPLEX HILL FORTS AND ISLAND STRONGHOLDS.

Judging by archaeological finds, they were great horsemen but, strangely, little evidence has been found to verify the wide use of the chariots that so often feature in Irish myths. Nor were they necessarily as destructive as the myths suggest: much Celtic warfare may have been ritualized, a matter of raiding for cattle and slaves rather than conquest and massacre.

A VIOLENT SOCIETY. IRISH MERCENARIES KNOWN AS KERNS SET FIRE TO A HOUSE AND CARRY OFF HOUSEHOLD GOODS AND ANIMALS, WHILE THE OCCUPANTS LAMENT THEIR ILL-FORTUNE

The unrestrained violence and cruelty of the Norsemen seems to have infected the Irish, since early medieval chronicles preserve many tales of mutilation and vicious revenges, within as well as between the two groups. The native Irish also imitated the Ostmen in making the axe their favoured weapon. The 12th-century author Gerald of Wales describes their 'old and evil custom' of carrying axes about with them as if they were staffs, so that, if an Irishman felt an impulse to do violence, he could satisfy it instantly.

Nevertheless the Irish were at first no match for the 12th-century Anglo-Norman intruders, with their armour, big horses and strong castles. But they learned quickly. Even before royal government began to weaken, Anglo-Normans and 'Old Irish' were making alliances, quarrelling and waging petty wars, in a fashion not so very different from the Celts a thousand years earlier. And they found willing helpers. Bands of native mercenaries, known as kerns, took employment wherever they could find it or simply plundered the country. Barefoot and lightly armed, they seem to have been as formidable in their way as the gallowglasses, armoured axemen from the Western Isles who began to settle in Ireland from the mid-13th century and fight for pay.

PATRICK SARSFIELD, the most gifted Irish commander of his generation, led an impressive resistance to William III's army which might have been even more effective if his royal master James II had possessed better nerves

This late medieval anarchy was gradually mastered by the soldiers of Tudor England, representing a completely new kind of centralized state and the latest in military technology – artillery, muskets and massed pikes deployed by infantry in close formation. Henry VIII's artillery destroyed Kildare's supremacy, and Elizabethan conquest and colonization, though irregularly pursued, seemed to have only one possible conclusion. This was recognized by an Irishman of political and military genius, Hugh O'Neill, Earl of Tyrone. Alone of Irish leaders, O'Neill quietly created a 'modern' army and, when forced into revolt, inflicted several heavy defeats on the over-confident English. For years he was able to hold out in his wild Ulster strongholds, waiting for Spanish help which arrived too late in the day and precipitated a final catastrophe.

In the 17th century, the Catholic Irish found their ablest commander in Patrick Sarsfield, who led the resistance to William III's forces after his own master, James II, had fled. Sarsfield was one of the thousands of 'Wild Geese' who left an English-dominated Ireland and fled abroad. Ireland subsequently produced many military men, fighting for different causes – the Duke of Wellington, Michael Collins, Field Marshal Montgomery – and also, in more recent times, some highly visible soldier- 'peacekeepers' in the service of the United Nations.

THE IRON DUKE, A SPLENDIDLY COMMANDING FIGURE, IS SHOWN ON THE BATTLEFIELD WITH BRITISH HUSSARS IN 1814. THE VICTOR OF WATERLOO, DUKE OF WELLINGTON, WAS BORN IN DUBLIN INTO THE LONG-ESTABLISHED WELLESLEY FAMILY

THE ANGLO-IRISH

DURING THE 18TH CENTURY THE GREAT ANGLO-IRISH
FAMILIES ENJOYED AN UNCHALLENGED SUPREMACY IN
BOTH POLITICS AND SOCIETY.

CONSTANCE GORE-BOOTH WAS PRESENTED
AT COURT – BUT, LATER, AS COUNTESS MARKIEVICZ,
TOOK PART IN THE EASTER RISING AND BECAME
THE FIRST WOMAN ELECTED (FOR SINN FEINN) TO
THE BRITISH HOUSE OF COMMONS

Though never as wealthy as the great landowners who dominated the English scene, they created a similar 'Augustan' culture, at once sociable, urbane and elegant. On their estates they built country houses in the approved classical style, filled with good pictures, fine furniture, silver and glass. As members of the sole political class they spent much of their time in the capital, sitting in Parliament, carrying out official functions, or dancing attendance on the Lord Lieutenant at Dublin Castle, the centre and symbol of royal authority. As a consequence Dublin prospered and expanded, acquiring the great public buildings appropriate to a capital, as well as the Georgian streets and squares for which it is still celebrated.

The Irish Parliament was dominated by the aristocracy, and in particular by a few magnates who effectively controlled large numbers of MPs. This meant that government by 'the Castle' could be carried on through mutually satisfactory arrangements that would later be branded as 'corruption' – although in this the Dublin parliament was no different from its British model at Westminster.

Moreover, ultimate power lay with Westminster, which affirmed its own supremacy by an Act of 1720. The Anglo-Irish only slowly acquired the confidence to challenge British domination. An early example was the furore that broke out over 'Wood's halfpence', a licence to supply Ireland with copper coins whose inordinate profits were earmarked for the king's mistress. Opposition to the project was intensified by the success of *The Drapier's Letters* (1724), written by Jonathan Swift, the Dean of St Patrick's Cathedral, and the government was forced to abandon the project.

Later agitation for Irish rights, led by Henry Grattan, was not unlike that of thirteen other colonies that lay across the Atlantic. And in fact the British disaster in America led directly to the recognition of Ireland as a separate kingdom in 1782 – the high point of Anglo-Irish aspiration during the golden age of Ascendancy. After the revolutionary agitations of the

SQUALOR AND RIOT WERE AS MUCH A PART OF
18TH-CENTURY LIFE AS THE ELEGANT STATE BALL
(OPPOSITE) OR THE AUGUSTAN ASSURANCE OF THE
MPS IN FRANCIS WHEATLEY'S GROUP PORTRAIT
ON PAGE 33. HERE, JOHN NIXON CREATES A DUBLIN
EQUIVALENT TO HOGARTH'S SCENES OF LONDON LIFE

1790s, the Act of Union ended the aspirations but proved relatively easy for the Anglo-Irish to accept. London replaced Dublin as the centre of their political and social ambitions, with unfortunate consequences for the Irish capital. And although 'the big house' remained a potent influence and a symbol of a graceful way of life, the new dispensation encouraged absentee landlordism with all its attendant problems and abuses.

A STATE BALL AT DUBLIN CASTLE, RECORDED BY AN ANONYMOUS ARTIST WHO HAS CAPTURED THE MIXTURE OF SPLENDOUR AND RESTRAINT THAT CHARACTERIZED SUCH PUBLIC OCCASIONS DURING THE 18TH CENTURY. DUBLIN CASTLE, HOME TO THE VICEROY, WAS THE CENTRE OF GOVERNMENT AND IRELAND'S COURT. VICEREGAL PATRONAGE, AND THE SOCIAL CACHET OF ATTENDANCE AT COURT, KEPT ANGLO-IRISH OPPOSITION TO GOVERNMENT POLICIES WITHIN BOUNDS

After the Union, agitation for national rights became a primarily Catholic affair – numerically, at any rate. One of the curiosities of Irish history is how prominent a role individual Anglo-Irish men and women continued to play in the Irish nationalist movement as politicians (Parnell), revolutionaries (the Gore-Booth sisters) and cultural revivalists (Douglas Hyde). Nevertheless the rise of nationalism, and its social and military consequences – the estate sold, the big house burned – would ultimately spell the end for the Anglo-Irish.

TRAVEL & TRAVELLERS

AFTER IRELAND'S FIRST SETTLERS CROSSED THE NARROW WATERS SEPARATING IT FROM SCOTLAND, THEY FOUND A THICKLY FORESTED COUNTRY, HARD – AND DANGEROUS – TO PENETRATE EXCEPT ALONG THE COASTLINE AND THE BANKS OF THE RIVERS.

The most convenient means of travel was by boat, and the sturdy, versatile currach came into use for coastal waters and for sea crossings at a very early date. Made from a framework of laths covered with hides (later replaced by tarred canvas), the currach was an unremarkable-looking craft with a distinctive uprising prow, but it was capable of transporting large loads and weathering strongly adverse conditions. A vessel built on similar principles was said to have carried the 6th-century St Brendan on his Atlantic voyage, and in 1976 Tim Severin made the ocean crossing in a replica of Brendan's craft.

IN THE SAME BOAT. In medieval countries, the most efficient way of travelling was by boat, avoiding dark and dangerous paths and the few badly maintained roads. These Connaught men are paddling a small boat, most likely a version of the hide-covered currach, well-suited to negotiating Ireland's many rivers

Although the Celts settled all over Ireland, conditions in the country are hinted at in the legend of the renegade who undertook to guide Queen Maeve's Connaught army on its march against his native Ulster. Suffering qualms of conscience, he led the Connaught men up and down the country, approaching but never entering Ulster; and Maeve, though eventually suspicious, was geographically ill-informed enough to accept assurances that they were on the right road! For centuries, Celtic roads can have been little more than dirt tracks, on which a stranger had to keep a sharp look-out for an ambush. However, matters improved slightly with the coming of Christianity and the growth of monastic settlements with guest-houses in which travellers could find shelter and protection.

Throughout the medieval period, riding on horseback was the preferred mode of travel for those who could afford it; possessions and merchandise went by packhorse. The lack of any effective central authority, and the general insecurity, prevented any significant advances until the Elizabethan conquest of Ireland. Then, despite the savage wars and punitive land transfers of the 17th century, conditions improved greatly, with better roads encouraging the use of carriages, stage-coaches and post-chaises. As in Britain, improved communications promoted the more sociable and urbane society of the

BELFAST TRAMS ON STANDBY AS WORKERS POUR OUT OF THE HARLAND AND WOLFF SHIPYARD IN THIS TURN-OF-THE-CENTURY PHOTOGRAPH. DURING THIS PERIOD BELFAST WAS IRELAND'S LEADING INDUSTRIAL CITY, WITH A HIGHER STANDARD OF LIVING AND BETTER AMENITIES THAN THE ELEGANT BUT RUN-DOWN DUBLIN

PROVINCIAL TRAVELLERS IN 1880, PREPARING TO LEAVE ON ONE OF BIANCONI'S GALWAY-CLIFDEN MAIL CARS. THESE SIDECARS NOW LOOK HUMBLE ENOUGH, BUT THE ESTABLISHMENT OF A NETWORK OF 'BIANS' MADE CHEAP RURAL TRAVEL AVAILABLE FOR THE FIRST TIME

18th century. A canal system, mail-coaches and the development of increasingly high-speed stage-coaches also paralleled the British experience; but many small places remained isolated until an Italian immigrant, Carlo Bianconi, set up his headquarters at Clonmel and built up a full-scale coaching network that made the modest but indispensable 'Bians' one of Ireland's most familiar sights.

Although the main railway routes out of Dublin were constructed in the early 1850s, it was a long time before remote areas, especially in the West, felt their influence. Suburban lines, omnibuses and trams quickened life in the city and enabled communities to live outside the centre. The motor car remained a luxury until well into the 20th century, making only a marginal impact on most people's lives, in fact it was the railway excursion and the bicycle that finally ended rural isolation for all but the islanders living off the west coast in Atlantic waters. All that has changed in recent times, and nowadays even the Aran Islands, once the very symbol of an older, untouched way of life, can be reached by means of regular air service and are visited by travellers from all over the world.

LIFE ON THE LAND

FOR MOST OF IRELAND'S HISTORY, THE OVERWHELMING MAJORITY OF HER PEOPLE LIVED CLOSE TO THE LAND, PLANTING AND HARVESTING OR GRAZING AND TENDING HERDS.

Yet this relationship was a surprisingly unstable one, in which the balance between arable and pastoral, owner and tenant, was tipped this way and that, often under the influence of political and social conflicts.

From early Celtic times livestock were unusually important. They were usefully mobile assets in a turbulent society, prestigious prizes of war and, more prosaically, sources of milk and butter, which were for centuries the staple foods in the Irish diet. Although the Normans effected some improvements in farming the parts of the east and south that they controlled, most of the people continued to live at subsistence level, threatened with actual starvation whenever harvests disappointed or violence destroyed their meagre resources. The depth of misery in which the poorest Irish lived – in rags, with hovels for homes – struck outside observers of several different nationalities.

The threat of famine, and utter destitution at the bottom of the social ladder, were common enough in most European countries until at least the 18th century; but Ireland's experience of them lasted even longer. For a time it seemed as if the worst was over. After the grim struggles of the 17th century, outwardly amiable relations between the Ascendancy landlords and their Catholic tenants were established surprisingly quickly. And after 1750 the standard of living rose, rural housing conditions improved and a turn in British economic policy enabled Irish farms to grow and export large quantities of grain.

But the population was already soaring, and in Ireland, unlike Britain, there were no factories and expanding industrial towns to absorb the excess. The huge increase in numbers meant that there were not enough houses, lands or work to go round. The tumbledown shack again became a common sight, while the land was divided and subdivided into ever-smaller one-crop plots. Ireland's rural economy was already in crisis by the 1840s when the potato harvest failed and 'the Great Hunger' began.

The Famine resulted in suffering, death and emigration, variously permutated, and scarred the Irish people in a fashion impossible to quantify. When it was over, farms had become more substantial, but only

IRISH FARM WORKERS. THEIR LONG-TAILED JACKETS AND TALL HATS MAKE A MISLEADINGLY PROSPEROUS IMPRESSION WHICH DISAPPEARS ON CLOSER INSPECTION OF THE PICTURE. BY THE TIME THIS PHOTOGRAPH WAS TAKEN (PERHAPS THE 1860s) THE FAMINE WAS OVER, BUT LIFE REMAINED HARD

continued emigration ensured the viability of the economy. In fact the 'golden stream' – the remittances sent back to their families by millions of emigrants – became a vital element in maintaining the old way of life in the homeland , especially in the impoverished west.

During the Famine, many landlords – some faced with bankruptcy, some glad of an excuse – evicted tenants who could not pay their rent. Resentments were nursed which broke out fiercely during the great agricultural recession of the 1870s. The Irish Land League harnessed tenant discontents in campaigns that speeded the decline of the Anglo-Irish landlord class and the social revolution which turned Ireland into a land of peasant proprietors. There were drawbacks, notably the small scale on which the new owners necessarily operated, and Irish agriculture remained relatively backward. But the passionate land-hunger of the peasants was at last satisfied as Ireland moved into the 20th century.

THE EJECTED FAMILY. For all its Victorian sentimentality, this painting by Erskin Nicol does achieve a certain emotive force, perhaps generated by our knowledge that this was a bitter experience shared by thousands of families

IRISH INDUSTRY

OUTSIDE OF THE NORTH, IRELAND HAS NEVER BEEN A HEAVILY INDUSTRIALIZED COUNTRY. UNTIL RECENTLY, MOST OF HER MANUFACTURES HAVE BEEN ON A SMALL SCALE, OFTEN REPRESENTING BY-PRODUCTS OF AGRICULTURAL ACTIVITIES.

In the past, some – wool, cotton, sugar, soap, flour, paper, glass – were commercially significant exports for a time, only to fall foul of restrictive British laws or industrial competition. However, in two manufacturing activities – distilling and brewing – Ireland has long been one of the world leaders. The art and craft of distilling was probably brought to Ireland by Continental monks during the early Christian centuries; and this led to the transformation of barley into *uisce beatha*, 'the water of life', later known as whiskey. Spelling distinguishes the labelling of Irish whiskey from Scotch whisky; the triple distillation of the Irish product (by contrast with its double distillation in Scotland) is said to be responsible for its mellower taste. No doubt it was already being home-produced in quantities by 1608, when Sir Thomas Phillipps took out the first official licence; and his works, Old Bushmills, became the oldest licensed distillery in the world. The

ILLICIT WHISKEY, CALLED POTEEN, WAS MADE BY SECRET STILLS ALL OVER THE COUNTRY. THE ONE IN THIS 19TH-CENTURY PHOTOGRAPH IS A STUDIO FAKE, BUT GIVES A PRETTY ACCURATE IDEA OF WHAT THE REAL THING LOOKED LIKE

manufacture of illicit liquor, known as poteen, remained an Irish tradition, but in its properly matured form whiskey became the water of life for multitudes at home and abroad.

Irish brewing has become (unfairly to other brands) almost synonymous with Guinness. Its extraordinary success story began in 1759 when Arthur Guinness, the son of a land steward, took over a brewery at St James's Gate in Dublin. Switching from ale to the thick, heavy 'porter' popular in England, Guinness came up with an even denser, 'extra stout' version now universally known as a Guinness, with its trademark dark body and creamy head. By the late 19th century Guinness's Dublin brewery was the largest in the world; since then, its famous product has remained astonishingly popular – assisted by consistently imaginative advertising

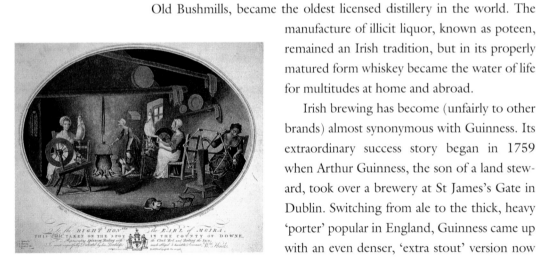

COTTAGE INDUSTRY is the appropriate title of this engraving (1791) by William Hinks, which shows linen yarn being spun, reeled and boiled. The linen industry was concentrated in the North

– and is now the basis of a world-wide business.

Northern Ireland's industrial expansion began with the widespread growing of flax, from which linen was spun and woven. Like other textiles, these were for a long time domestic industries, carried out by smallholders working in their cottages to supplement their incomes. Linen manufactures boosted the local economy, encouraging the growth

of Belfast even before the advent of powered machinery drove workers – many of them women – into the factories and turned them from country folk into city dwellers.

The industrialization of the North was above all accomplished by the shipyards which grew up on Belfast's river Lurgan. The pioneer firm was Harland and Wolff, which originated in the late 1850s; another ship-building giant, Workman Clark, began operations twenty years later. Among other things, Harland and Wolff were famous in their day as the builders of 'superliners' for the White Star Line, including the ill-fated *Titanic*. Like other 'old' industries, shipbuilding began a long-drawn-out decline after the First World War. The linen industry, too, suffered, especially after the introduction of synthetic materials, and eventually only a few specialist factories survived. Irish industry was left in the doldrums until recent times, when 'high-tech' operations began to create a very different sort of 'post-industrial' society.

THE TITANIC LEAVES BELFAST ON HER TRIALS IN THE SPRING OF 1912. BUILT BY HARLAND AND WOLFF AND BELIEVED TO BE UNSINKABLE, THE 'TITANIC' HIT AN ICEBERG ON HER MAIDEN VOYAGE AND SANK WITH GREAT LOSS OF LIFE

THE SPORTING LIFE

WHEN, AS A YOUNG MAN, THE IRISH HERO CUCHULAINN FIRST SET OUT FROM HOME, HE TOOK WITH HIM A HURLING STICK AND BALL TO WHILE AWAY THE TIME BETWEEN ADVENTURES. SINCE STORIES ABOUT CUCHULAINN DATE BACK TO THE EARLY CENTURIES AD, HURLING CAN CLAIM TO BE THE OLDEST OF IRISH SPORTS.

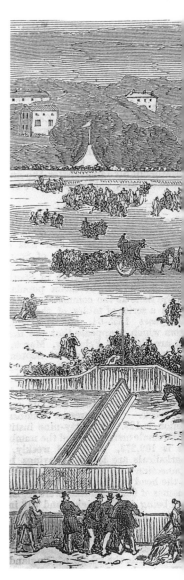

Like many early games, it was often played with murderous enthusiasm, prompting a medieval statute decreeing that 'the commons of the land of Ireland. . . use not henceforth the games which are called hurling, with great clubs and ball upon the ground, from which great evils and maims have arisen'. The statute was evidently ignored, and hurling was still being played in front of large crowds – and occasionally degenerating into a riot – in the 18th century.

Hurling is a hockey-like game, now played fifteen-a-side with a very broad, curved stick and a small, hard leather ball. The skills involved were admired by a curious visitor, a 17th-century London bookseller named Dunton, who described how 'you may sometimes see one of the gamesters carry the ball tossing it for 40 or 50 yards in spite of all the adverse players; and when he is likely to lose it, he generally gives it a great stroke to drive it towards the goal'.

A TENSE, STILL MOMENT IN THE ULTRA-FAST SPORT OF HURLING. THE PLAYERS ARE WAITING FOR THE BALL TO BE THROWN IN BY A VISITING CELEBRITY – MICHAEL COLLINS, THE IRISH LEADER WHO WAS TO DIE IN AN AMBUSH AT THE HANDS OF FELLOW-REPUBLICANS. THE MATCH IS BEING PLAYED AT CROKE PARK, STILL THE VENUE OF HURLING AND OTHER GAELIC SPORTS FINALS

After falling out of favour during the 19th century, hurling was one of the sports to be revived by the Gaelic Athletic Association. This innocuous-sounding organization, founded at Thurles in 1884, was one of the main agents of an intense cultural nationalism that aimed to revive the Gaelic language and 'native' traditions. The GAA was remarkably successful, building up a network of local clubs, and it is even now a power in sporting Ireland. As well as hurling and camogie (a women's version of the game), the GAA promoted handball and Gaelic football. Like other forms of the game, Gaelic football seems to have originated as a mass free-for-all; and although its rules have been refined over the years, and the number of players on each side reduced to fifteen, it has remained a singularly robust form of the contest, combining elements of rugby and association football to create a tough, fast-moving spectacle.

Although not exclusively Irish, horse-racing can only be described as a traditional national sport. The Irish passion for horses is centuries old: the Curragh, still Ireland's most famous course, was already popular for stabling and racing in the 17th century. The GAA's hostility to 'foreign'

THE IRISH GRAND NATIONAL, AS STAGED AT CORK IN 1869. THIS PREMIER
STEEPLE-CHASE EVENT IS NOW HELD AT FAIRYHOUSE, WHILE THE PRINCIPAL FLAT
RACING COURSE IS THE CURRAGH. THERE ARE MANY OTHER RACECOURSES AND
EVENTS, INCLUDING THE UNIQUE LAYTOWN MEETING, RUN ON THE BEACH

'PART OF OUR HERITAGE'. PAINTED ON THE
SIDE OF A HOUSE IN BELFAST, THIS MURAL INDICATES
THAT THE POLITICAL ROLE OF GAELIC SPORTS IS STILL
VERY MUCH TO THE FORE IN THE NORTH, HELPING
TO DEFINE ONE OF TWO VERY DIFFERENT VERSIONS
OF WHAT IT MEANS TO BE IRISH

(code for British) sports persisted well into
the 20th century, but fears that their introduction might undermine Gaelic sports has proved
unfounded. Among others, association football, rugby, cycling, golf, boxing and grey-
hound racing have attracted large followings,
and there is large-scale public participation in a
variety of sports and pastimes. Both the Irish and their visitors tend to be
passionate golfers and the abundance of rivers, lakes and suitable coast-
lines has made Ireland ideal for inland and sea-fishing. And of course,
in admired figures such as George Best, Stephen Roche and Barry
McGuigan, Ireland has produced at least her share of world-famous
sports personalities.

THE LOVE OF MUSIC

THE IRISH HAVE LONG BEEN THOUGHT OF AS AN INTEN-
SELY MUSICAL PEOPLE, AND THERE IS A GOOD DEAL OF
EVIDENCE FROM THE PAST TO SUPPORT THE IDEA.

Superbly made and well-preserved bronze instruments have been
recovered from Ireland's bogs, perhaps deliberately thrown in as a worthy tribute to a local spirit or god. There have been both Celtic and
pre-Celtic finds, evidently representing a long prehistoric tradition.

MERRY-MAKING AMONG FRIENDS AND NEIGHBOURS. NICHOLAS CROWLEY'S
PAINTING OF AN EARLY 19TH-CENTURY GATHERING CAPTURES THE CONVIVIAL HIGH
SPIRITS AND INFORMALITY OF THE OCCASION. MEN AND WOMEN OF ALL AGES MAKE
THEMSELVES AT HOME, DANCING TO THE LIVELY MUSIC

By Celtic times the harp was already the queen of instruments, and master-harpers were privileged beings whom chiefs delighted to honour. There was little change after the Anglo-Norman invasion; although the authorities were clearly inclined to eliminate this symbol of Gaelic culture, the new lords went their own way, and proved eager to take over a native tradition that entailed hearing themselves praised, each in his own court, in grand Homeric terms. The high skill of 12th-century musicians was confirmed by the chronicler Gerald of Wales, in most other respects a harsh critic of the Irish. Music was the one sphere in which they were really diligent, he conceded, and in that art they were superior to all other peoples. Unlike the British, they favoured quick and lively airs, which were performed harmoniously in concert on several instruments, and with a deceptive ease that made the result a perfect example of 'the art that conceals art'.

The Irish harp was a small, portable instrument with a distinctive shape (notably the 'pillar' at the front, curved instead of upright as on a modern harp); it was played with fingernails which had been grown especially long for the purpose. A few early examples have survived, including the Harp of Brian Boru (actually some centuries later) in Trinity College, Dublin. Other early instruments included one with strings, called the tympanum, and the pipes, similar to the better-known bagpipes of Scotland.

Tudor administrators and colonists were less friendly than their predecessors to Irish traditions, but the old ways persisted. As late as 1610 the writer-soldier Barnaby Rich declared that 'the Irish have harpers, and these are so reverenced among them that in the time of rebellion they will forbear to hurt either their persons or their goods. . . and every great man in the country hath his rhymer and his harper'. But the drastic 17th-century events which ruined the Catholic landowning class also doomed the poets and harpers supported by their bounty. The harpers became itinerants, sometimes even reduced to living by manual labour. Since no one thought of writing them down until it was too late, most of their traditional melodies were lost, although 'the last of the bards', the blind Turlough Carolan (1670-1738), became famous during his lifetime, and his own compositions, curiously blending traditional and fashionable Italian elements, have survived.

Although they had come down in the world, the harpers represented an aloof, aristocratic tradition. The common people had their own

THE MAGIC OF THE FIDDLE IS THE SUBJECT OF CHARLES HUNT'S PAINTING 'PADDY'S COURTSHIP' (1896). EASY TO CARRY FROM PLACE TO PLACE, THE FIDDLE COULD DO THE WORK OF AN ENTIRE BAND OR, AS HERE, COULD BE MADE TO SPEAK ELOQUENTLY FROM HEART TO HEART

music, performed on the pipes and increasingly, from the 17th century, on the violin, almost universally known (then and now) as the fiddle; flutes and whistles, and later the concertina, also became part of popular music-making. The fiddle's ability to range from plaintiveness to rhythmic frenzy made it the most suitable instrument for most gatherings, especially where there were jigs, reels and other dances to be performed.

There are curiously few early references to dancing, although Fynes Morrison, a 16th-century traveller and government agent, observed that the Irish 'delight much in danc-ing, using no art of slow measures or lofty galliards, but only country dancing'. These performances sound as though they related to distant pagan traditions, for 'they dance about a fire commonly in the midst of a room hold-ing withes in their hands, and by certain strains drawing one another into the fire; and also the matachine dance, with naked swords, which they make to meet in divers postures.'

By the 18th century there could be no doubt about it. Dancing was one of the most popular Irish pastimes, cheerful but also cheap, and enthusiastically practiced on Sundays and at weddings, wakes and fairs, in taverns and out in the fields. Another English traveller, Arthur Young, declared that 'Dancing is very general among the poor people, almost universal in every cabin'. In spite of which there was noth-ing wild and careless in the Irish approach to dancing: the 18th century was the heyday of the peripatetic dancing master, touring from village to village and living on the sixpences he collected in return for teaching the inhabitants all the latest steps.

During the same period, the upper class patronized the cosmopolitan musical culture, and to some effect: it was in Dublin, on 13 April 1742, that Handel's *Messiah* received its first performance. But in Ireland, as in other parts of Europe, the Romantic movement began to stir an inter-est in the past, expressed in occasions such as the Belfast Harp Festival of 1792, and in historical novels, nostalgic poetry and folklore research. The Irish folklorists were only partly successful in recording fading traditions, especially as the task was complicated by the rapid substitu-tion of English for Irish Gaelic. Popular balladry often incorporated some Irish cadences, although in time it became commercialized and verged on self-parody. Nostalgia, and also sentimentality, made an early appearance in the *Irish Melodies* of the poet Thomas Moore

LOST GLORIES, REAL AND IMAGINARY, ARE EVOKED IN THIS PAGE ILLUSTRATING ONE OF THOMAS MOORE'S 'IRISH MELODIES'. THE ARTIST, DANIEL MACLISE, WAS, LIKE MOORE, AN IRISHMAN WHO MADE A SUCCESSFUL CAREER IN ENGLAND, AT LEAST PARTLY BASED ON THE NOSTALGIC APPEAL OF THE CELTIC PAST TO ROMANTICS EVERYWHERE. AS BOTH SONG AND ILLUSTRATION SUGGEST, THE HARP WAS ALREADY A PRIME SYMBOL OF IRISHNESS

(1779-1852), whose verses set to 18th-century airs were enormously popular. They included *The Last Rose of Summer*, *The Minstrel Boy* and a celebrated lament for past glories:

The harp that once, thro' Tara's halls,
The soul of music shed,
Now hangs as mute on Tara's walls,
As if that soul were fled.

The Irish contribution to 'serious' music has been a significant one; the most distinguished figures include the composer John Field, the world-famous tenor John McCormack and, more recently, the flautist James Galway. Traditional Irish forms have caught the world's imagination through the performances of the Chieftains and the musical *Riverdance*. But the most surprising musical development has been the number of Irish artists using modern forms and making an international impact – to name only a few, the blues performer Van Morrison, Bob Geldof and the Boomtown Rats, the group U2, and the controversial radical-feminist singer Sinead O'Connor.

IRISH FOLK MUSIC EXPERIENCED AN UNEXPECTED REVIVAL IN THE 1960S, THANKS TO TALENTED GROUPS SUCH AS THE DUBLINERS, THE CLANCY BROTHERS AND THE CHIEFTAINS. OFTEN SKILFULLY ADAPTED TO MODERN TASTES AND CONDITIONS, THEIR MUSIC APPEALED TO AUDIENCES IN MANY PARTS OF EUROPE AND AMERICA

LORD OF THE DANCE is the title of a popular musical and also an apt description of its star, Michael Flatley. A phenomenal revival of Irish dancing began at Dublin's Point Theatre in April 1994, when Flatley and Jean Butler led a seven-minute performance in the interval of the Eurovision Song Contest. Warmly received, it gave rise to the immensely successful shows Riverdance and Lord of the Dance

MYTH MAGIC & FOLKLORE

LEFT: The Giant's Causeway, County Antrim
RIGHT: The Dance of the litte people, by William
Holmes Sullivan

THE BURREN, County Clare, with Poulnabrone Dolmen

IRELAND HAS A RICH HERITAGE OF MYTHICAL
LORE, OF A KIND FOUND NOWHERE ELSE.
ITS ANNALS DESCRIBE HOW, LONG AGO, GODS,
HEROES AND LOVERS LIVED OUT THEIR HIGH
DESTINIES ON IRISH SOIL

MONKS, GODS & HEROES

CELTIC SOCIETY EXPANDED TO COVER VAST AREAS OF NORTHERN EUROPE BETWEEN ABOUT 600 BC AND AD 400. YET THE HISTORICAL IMPORTANCE OF THE CELTS IS EASY TO UNDERESTIMATE BECAUSE THEY LEFT BEHIND ALMOST NO WRITTEN RECORDS.

Their thoughts and beliefs can only be inferred from the observations made by Greek and Roman writers, from carved figures and other archaeological remains, and from Celtic oral traditions, which were of course recorded centuries after the real or imaginary events they describe.

In Ireland such oral accounts were written down from the 6th century AD by monastic scribes. They form a series of stirring tales of the settlement of the island, its larger-than-life heroes and lovers, and the fated combats and wars of a pre-Christian Ireland. Remarkably, the monks did not intrude Christian elements into the stories, leaving them saturated with pagan supernatural elements; and this suggests that the scribes were faithful recorders of what they knew or were told.

By contrast, no coherent account of religion among the pre-Christian Irish has survived, if such a thing ever existed. It seems reasonable to suppose that Irish religion was not very different from that of the Celts in Britain and elsewhere, with its druid-priests, sacred groves, severed-head cult, human sacrifices, and belief in a life continuing after death in another world. Many of these are in fact alluded to in the myth-cycles recorded by Irish monks. But a striking local variation was the Celtic interpretation of Newgrange and other Neolithic tombs as entrances to the Otherworld below; the limits of the two worlds were never completely impassable, and became frighteningly fluid at Samhain (1 November), a feast-day which is still celebrated as Hallowe'en.

As written down by the monks, the major Irish myths are prose tales, now preserved in manuscripts dating from the 12th century. Most of the tales belong to three great cycles. The Mythological Cycle, mainly recorded in *The Book of Invasions*, traces the beings who settled in Ireland from the time of the Flood, including Parthelon from Greece, the evil Fermorians, the Fir Bolg, and the Tuatha de Dannan, divine beings who were driven underground by the Gaels. The Ulster Cycle recounts the wars between Ulster and Connaught, while the Fenian Cycle describes the adventures of Finn MacCool and his warband, the Fianna.

THE COURT OF THE GODS, PRESIDED OVER BY ITS KING, LUGH. THIS FANCIFUL 19TH-CENTURY ILLUSTRATION CREATES A CELTIC PANTHEON WHICH IT VIEWS SEMI-HUMOROUSLY, MUCH AGAINST THE GRAIN OF THE ORIGINAL NARRATIVES

THREE-FACED STONE HEAD FROM CORLECK, COUNTY CAVAN; PROBABLY LATE BC OR EARLY AD. MANY SIMILAR HEADS HAVE BEEN FOUND IN THE BRITISH ISLES AND ELSEWHERE, REFLECTING THE CELTIC CULT OF THE SEVERED HEAD AND SKULLS, AND THE GREAT MAGICAL SIGNIFICANCE OF THE NUMBER THREE. BY CONTRAST, REPRESENTATIONS OF THE FULL HUMAN FIGURE ARE RELATIVELY INFREQUENT IN CELTIC ART

THE HILL OF TARA, County Meath. In
Irish myth this was the seat of Irish god-kings,
and later it was associated with the historical
high kings. The site is archaeologically complex,
having been occupied, and evidently regarded
as sacred, at least since Neolithic times

The Celtic myths evoke a world of heroic values, embodied in doomed but dauntless warriors, that resembles the world of Achilles, Hector and Ajax in Homer's *Iliad*. But whereas Homer's world is visibly that of human beings, however much god- and fate-haunted, the Irish myths take place in a more fanciful, magical dimension; their heroes are mortals who can be destroyed but are in most other respects like supernatural beings, capable of weird transformations and impossible feats that will leave indelible marks on the very landscape of Ireland. Yet the stories also carry an unusually strong and convincing sense of the blind power of sexual passions (especially the sexual passions of women), and of their tragic consequences in ruthless loves, relentless hatreds, dishonour, flight and murder. Although they can be related to the cycles of other lands, these Irish myths have a definite and distinctive ambience.

THE LIFE & DEATH OF CUCHULAINN

THE BEST-KNOWN STORIES IN THE ULSTER CYCLE BELONG TO A GROUP KNOWN AS THE CATTLE RAID OF COOLEY. THE HUMDRUM-SOUNDING TITLE REFLECTS THE VALUE PUT ON CATTLE AS SPOILS OF WAR BY THE CELTIC WARRIOR-ARISTOCRACY; BUT THE BULLS IN THIS STORY ARE NO ORDINARY CATTLE.

It begins one night with Queen Maeve of Connaught lying in bed with her husband Ailill. Comparing their possessions, they find they are well-matched – except that Ailill has a huge white bull, the Findbennach. Maeve, a woman of enormous ambition and sexual appetite, cannot bear to be Ailill's inferior in any respect, and arranges to acquire the only comparable animal, the Donn or Brown Bull of Ulster, offering the owner a large reward which includes her own favours. But when Maeve's men arrive to collect the bull, they are overheard boasting noisily that they would have carried off the bull whether or not the owner agreed. Furious, he hides the Donn away instead of handing it over.

THE GIANT'S CAUSEWAY HAS, RATHER SURPRISINGLY, BEEN KNOWN TO THE WIDER WORLD ONLY SINCE THE 18TH CENTURY, ABOUT THE TIME WHEN THIS PRINT WAS MADE. ITS BASALT COLUMNS ARE THE REMAINS OF ANCIENT VOLCANIC LAVA, BUT IN IRISH MYTH THEY ARE STEPS IN A CAUSEWAY TO SCOTLAND, LAID DOWN BY FINN MACCOOL

Maeve's response is to invade Ulster. Its warriors cannot resist the Connaught men, since they have been smitten with weakness as the result of a curse (another story in which boasting – the warrior's vice – has fatal results). Only one man is exempt, but he is Cuchulainn, a mighty warrior capable of taking on Maeve's entire army.

Cuchulainn's past has fitted him for this supreme test. Even as a child he was a prodigy of strength. Originally named Setanta, he set out for the court of King Conchobar, who is variously said to have been his uncle and his foster-father. On his way Setanta fought off a force of 150 young warriors who served Conchobar. At the court, an intruder, he was attacked by a ferocious guard-dog belonging to the smith Culann, which he killed by flinging his hurling ball down the creature's throat. When Culann asked woefully who would guard him from then onwards, Setanta promised that he would do it; and so he became Cuchulainn, 'the Hound of Culann'. Later, still a child, he chose his own destiny. Hearing a prophecy that a boy who took up arms on a certain day would become famous but would not live long, Cuchulainn asked Conchobar for weapons. After breaking fifteen sets of arms, he took up specially made arms that had been intended for the king himself, and then went out and slew a band of Conchobar's most dangerous enemies.

Many tales are told of Cuchulainn; like Odysseus and Aeneas, he even ventures into the Otherworld. But unlike the classical heroes, he is more than human: seven fingered, and with seven pupils in each eye and a brow from which shines forth a 'hero light'; able to turn round inside his own skin; hideously transformed and blood-crazed in battle; and, for good measure, armed with a variety of magic weapons. Evidently Cuchulainn is invincible; but, as a hero, he is also doomed.

In the war between Connaught and Ulster, Cuchulainn slays huge numbers of Maeve's followers, and the queen is only able to destroy him by a resort to magic. She does this by arranging encounters in which he cannot avoid violating certain binding personal tabus; like many other mythical heroes, he is innocently self-doomed. A series of evil portents occur as he prepares for battle, and

A CELTIC CROWN, OF A KIND CERTAINLY FIT FOR A KING. THE 'PETRIE CROWN' IS PART OF A BRONZE CEREMONIAL HEADDRESS, BEAUTIFULLY SHAPED AND PATTERNED, WHICH DATES FROM ABOUT THE 1ST CENTURY AD. ORIGINALLY IT WOULD HAVE INCLUDED SEVERAL UPSTANDING BRONZE HORNS

THE DEATH OF A FRIEND. When Cuchulainn's sworn friend Ferdia took service with Queen Maeve, the two were forced to fight. Cuchulainn, the victor, carries Ferdia across the river so that he may lie with his own kind

finally he meets the Washer at the Ford, a death-goddess in the form of a loud-lamenting maiden; her cleansing of a hero's arms and armour in a stream presages his imminent death in battle. Nevertheless Cuchulainn again defends the kingdom of Ulster against the hosts of Connaught. Wounded, he ties himself to a stone pillar so that he may die on his feet. Only when his hero-light fades and the death-crow descends and perches on his shoulder are the men of Connaught confident enough to advance and cut off his head.

The story of the great bulls takes a curious turn which ends the conflict between the Irish kingdoms. Having seized the Brown Bull of Ulster, Maeve sends it into Connaught, and on entering its new territory it lets out a great roar. Believing itself challenged, the white bull begins an epic fight that rages all round Ireland. Finally the Donn is victorious, scattering pieces of his mangled rival in every direction; but the effort has been too much for him, and he dies of exhaustion.

SYMBOL OF SACRIFICE. Oliver Sheppard's bronze sculpture, 'The Death of Cuchulainn' shows the hero tied to a stone pillar so that he may die on his feet, defending Ulster against overwhelming numbers. The figure now stands in the General Post Office, Dublin, where it symbolizes the sacrifices made during the Easter Rising of 1916, when the GPO served as the rebel headquarters

Cuchulainn is the supreme youthful hero of the Ulster Cycle, but two other mighty men dwell at Conchobar MacNessa's court at Emain Macha. One, Ferghus, was king before Conchobar, but gave up the throne to become the lover of Conchobar's mother, Nessa; evidently there was little sacrifice involved, since he shares the frequently expressed Celtic preference for a free life of hunting and feasting. He and another great Ulster hero, Conall Cernach, are unwittingly involved in an act of treachery perpetrated by Conchobar, and are so outraged that they defect to Connaught. After war breaks out, Ulster is saved by Ferghus's paternal feelings towards Cuchulainn, whom he has sworn never to fight; when Cuchulainn appears on the field of battle Ferghus and his followers quit the war.

Ferghus's appetites are more than human, and ritually expressed by the magic number seven: at one meal he can eat seven pigs, seven deer and seven cows, while emptying seven vats of liquor; and he needs seven women to satisfy him sexually. Not surprisingly, he is said to have the strength of seven hundred men. Like Conchobar, he has been one of Maeve's husbands, and such multiple regal couplings, like the gargantuan nature of the heroes, differentiate the chief figures in Irish myths from those of, for example, the Homeric epics: Achilles and Odysseus, however mighty, are fully human, whereas Ferghus, Maeve and the rest are humanized versions of Celtic gods. But in one area – their love stories – the kings and heroes prove to be all-too-human.

A ROYAL PALACE once stood here, at Emain Macha, now known as Navan Fort, Armagh. It was the seat of King Conchobar, defended against the hosts of Connaught by Cuchulainn. Excavations have revealed evidence of substantial building over a long period during the 1st millennium BC, culminating in a huge structure believed to have been of religious rather than political significance

THE QUEEN'S TOMB. The flat-topped hill of Knocknarea, near Sligo, is crowned by a huge cairn of stones. These are said to mark the tomb of Queen Maeve, or Medbh, whose jealousy led to the war between Connaught and Ulster, and the deeds and death of Cuchulainn. The cairn probably does cover a grave, believed to be much older than the Celtic legend

TALES OF LOVE & DEATH

A NUMBER OF CULTURES HAVE CREATED MYTHS IN WHICH PASSION IS SHOWN AS A SOCIALLY DESTRUCTIVE FORCE, UNDERMINING TRADITIONAL LOYALTIES AND CAUSING SACRED OATHS AND OBLIGATIONS TO BE VIOLATED.

In the Irish myths this malign relationship is expressed quite directly, but the actions of the erring lovers are treated with an unmistakable sympathy. The numbers three and seven occur again and again in Celtic myth. Three is especially associated with the sacred, and triads of gods and goddesses are very common. So it is appropriate that the best-known love stories feature the eternal triangle – typically one in which a powerful older man has a claim on a beautiful woman whose love for a younger man leads to disaster.

The tale of Deirdre and Naoise is unusually restrained and realistic in its handling of events. King Conchobar and his Red Branch Knights are carousing in the house of a noble lady, Fedlimid, when the druid Cathbadh is moved to prophecy: Fedlimid's daughter Deirdre, still in her mother's womb, will become a grey-eyed, yellow-haired woman whose beauty will cause the death of many Ulster warriors. Conchobar's men clamour to have her killed, but the king decides to foster her in a secret place until she is old enough to marry him. As the time approaches, Deirdre sees Conchobar skinning a calf in the snow while a raven drinks its blood. She tells her companion that she would wish to love a man with hair like the raven's, cheek like the blood and body like the snow's – not a man with the white hair of the now-ageing Conchobar. Her companion tells Deirdre of such a man: Naoise, one of the king's knights.

Deirdre seeks out Naoise, finds the young man unwilling to betray his master, but shames him into yielding. Deirdre, Naoise and his two brothers flee the court and move from place to place, eventually taking refuge in Scotland – where, however, the king's attentions make their situation increasingly dangerous. When Conchobar sends a message promising to forgive the lovers, Deirdre senses treachery but Naoise is convinced by the guarantees offered in good faith by his friend, the hero Ferghus, and the fugitives decide to return to Emain Macha.

MOMENT OF TERROR. IN W.B YEATS' PLAY DEIRDRE, THE LOVERS DEIRDRE AND NAOISE TRY TO RELAX BY PLAYING A GAME OF CHESS AFTER RETURNING TO EMAIN MACHA, BELIEVING THAT KING CONCHOBAR HAS FINALLY FORGIVEN THEIR ELOPEMENT. HOWEVER, THEIR ILLUSIONS ARE SOON SHATTERED – A MOMENT CAPTURED BRILLIANTLY IN THIS PHOTOGRAPH OF THE FAMOUS ACTRESS MRS PATRICK CAMPBELL, WHO PLAYED THE PART OF DEIRDRE IN 1907-08

Ferghus is lured away to a feast, and Conchobar commits the act of treachery that causes the hero to defect to Connaught: he orders the execution of Naoise and his brothers. Conchobar's followers only obey when a minor king, Eoghan, takes Naoise's sword and, with a single sweep, beheads all three men.

Conchobar holds Deirdre for a year, during which she never smiles or raises her head. Finally he asks her whom she hates most in the world. 'Yourself, surely,' she answers, 'and Eoghan, son of Duracht.' Then, decrees Conchobar, intent on completing his revenge, she must go and live with Eoghan. But when she is mounted behind Eoghan in his chariot and Conchobar taunts her, she flings herself against a rock so that she shatters her head and dies.

In the Celtic myths, gods and goddesses, human beings and the natural world are close to one another and the boundaries between them are fluid. 'Shape-shifting' is common. It is fearful when a goddess changes from a beauty to a hag, but touching in the story of the god Midhir, who loves a mortal: after a thousand years apart they are united and, transformed into swans, fly away together. The Irish were especially sensitive to the beauty of swans, evoked in poetic

POINT OF DEPARTURE. While Irish narratives are curiously specific, they are not necessarily accurate, in describing the settings of myths. This is Cushendun beach, from which the lovers Deirdre and Naoise, along with Naoise's brothers sailed for Scotland to escape from King Conchobar

DIVINE CONTOUR. THIS MOUNTAIN IN COUNTY KERRY IS CALLED DA CHICH ANNAN, 'THE BREASTS OF ANU', FOR REASONS WHICH THE PHOTOGRAPH MAKES PLAIN. ANU (OR DANU OR DANA) WAS A MOTHER-GODDESS AND PERHAPS 'THE MOTHER OF THE IRISH GODS', THOSE MYTHICAL COLONIZERS OF IRELAND KNOWN AS TUATHA DE DANNAN. SHE WAS VIRTUALLY IDENTIFIED WITH IRELAND AND THE IRISH PEOPLE, WHOSE PROSPERITY AND FERTILITY SHE ENSURED

A BED FOR LOVERS. Dolmens such as this are the remains of prehistoric tombs. But in old Ireland they were often called 'Diarmaid's Beds'. Having fled from the wrath of Finn MacCool, the lovers Diarmaid and Grainne were advised by a friendly god that for a year and a day they should never spend more than a night in each place Each dolmen was believed to be a bed put up by Diarmaid, and there were said to be 366 in Ireland

tales like that of the Children of Lir, doomed to wander the waters for nine hundred years.

Another set of stories mixing heroic deeds with romantic tragedy is the Fenian Cycle. Its chief personage, Finn MacCool, is like Cuchulainn and Ferghus in being a warrior's fantasy, performing deeds so gargantuan that some have suspected that a sly humour underlies the derring-do. But Finn is also the chief of the Fianna, an elite corps dedicated to the defence of Ireland; and he is the deceived participant in a classic love-triangle. He is betrothed to the beautiful Grainne, but she falls in love with Diarmaid, one of the Fianna. Like Deirdre, Grainne makes the first advances, overcomes the young man's reluctance, and flees with him.

More fortunate than Deirdre, Grainne is helped by her foster-father, the god Oenghus, who even takes on Diarmaid's form to lure away Finn's men. Eventually Finn is persuaded to pardon the lovers, who settle down and have five children. But later the hero's resentment boils up again and he lures Diarmaid to a boar-hunt, knowing through a prophecy that this is how Diarmaid will die; in one version Finn has the power to heal Diarmaid's wound but hesitates until it is too late.

The episode of Finn's treachery may have been a late addition, perhaps designed to give the story a tragic dimension. It remained a great popular favourite in the folklore that grew out of the myths, and the dolmens all over Ireland came to be identified as 'Diarmaid's Beds', each believed to have sheltered the fleeing lovers for a night. Folklore identified other mythical happenings with ancient sites, and also kept alive many pagan beliefs. This is at first sight surprising in view of Irish Christian devotion, but the beliefs in question were rendered harmless by their lack of any coherent spiritual meaning; they consequently presented no serious threat to the Church and could be more or less tolerated as manifestations of absurd and even endearing 'superstitions'.

However, leprechauns and other 'little people' were not always as harmless as they have become in modern popularized versions. The banshee's wailing was heard in households where a death was about to occur, and 'the fairies' stole a 'tithe' of farmers' produce and were notorious kidnappers, leaving behind a changeling child or a look-alike corpse. In time, such beliefs dwindled in many places, but in the 1900s J. M. Synge found that fairies were 'more numerous in Mayo than in any other county'; and there were few doubters in the remote Aran Islands, where old men 'grew nervous about the fairies' as they contemplated a night walk home across the sandhills.

THE IRISH ARTS

LEFT: Monasterboice: Detail of the shaft of the Cross of Muiredach, County Louth

RIGHT: Woodcutters resting in a Woodland Glade

THE PIER; Painting by Jack B. Yeats

IRELAND'S ARTISTIC ACHIEVEMENTS MIRROR
THE VARIOUSNESS OF HER HISTORY,
INCLUDING SUCH TREASURES AS ORNAMENTS,
OF PAGAN GOLD, PRECIOUS ILLUMINATED
MANUSCRIPTS, HIGH CROSSES AND MODERN
MASTER PAINTINGS

PATTERNS ON STONE & METAL

IRISH ART, LIKE IRISH HISTORY, BEGINS RELATIVELY LATE ON THE HUMAN TIME-SCALE. IN ITS EARLIEST KNOWN PHASES, ALL THE WORKS THAT WERE FASHIONED ARE BELIEVED TO HAVE SERVED SOME UTILITARIAN PURPOSE.

This is obvious in the case of pottery and flint tools and weapons, and probably applies even to examples of abstract ornamentation. Their constituents (pattern, balance, proportion and so on) are undoubtedly expressions of the aesthetic sense; but the end product is likely to have had some religious or magical significance, perhaps as visual mantras protecting the dead or propitiating their spirits. As in ancient Egypt and other societies where belief in an afterlife has been strong, the building of

ABSTRACT ART, created over 5,000 years ago. This impressive large kerbstone is typical of many of Ireland's stone monuments and stands outside the entrance to the burial chamber at Newgrange, one of Ireland's famous Neolithic monuments. Images of whorls and diamonds cover the surface of the stone in an abstract pattern

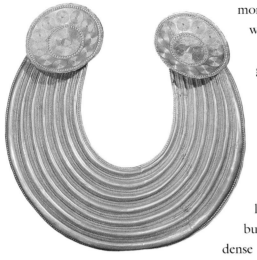

monumental tombs and the practice of art-magic would have been strictly utilitarian activities.

The carvings that appear on the stones of the great Neolithic tombs in the Boyne Valley and elsewhere lend themselves to such an interpretation. Spirals, loops, diamonds, triangles, squares, zigzags and chevrons are cut into the pillars and slabs that line the passages and burial chambers, and also into the kerbstones that ring the tomb mounds. A particularly well-known example is the large stone which stands at the entrance to the burial chamber at Newgrange; it is covered with a dense pattern of whorls and diamonds that follows the irregularities of the surface, producing an effect resembling an ammonite-like fossil.

GOLD FOR GREATNESS. THE GLENINSHEEN GOLD COLLAR COULD ONLY HAVE BEEN MADE FOR A PERSON OF HIGH RANK. IN ADDITION TO ITS INTRINSIC VALUE, IT IS A SUPERB EXAMPLE OF THE METALWORKER'S ART, EMPLOYING SEVERAL DIFFERENT TECHNIQUES

The makers of this 'Boyne Valley art' remain unknowable, yet they can be regarded as the founders of a great tradition. Perhaps dating as far back as 3000 BC, their pattern-making, asymmetrical yet balanced, includes many features that would persist in Irish art for millennia.

Metalworking was practised from about 2000 BC in Ireland, where the deposits of copper and gold became the basis for extensive production and exporting. Thanks to the malleability of copper and gold, smiths could use them to make a wide range of useful or purely ornamental artefacts, beginning with sheet-metal objects such as lunulae (crescent-shaped objects, possibly worn round the neck) and flat discs. Techniques improved greatly down the centuries, and the Irish became skilled at soldering, twisting and hammering metal, mastering repoussé work (reliefs fashioned by hammering the metal from the underside) and producing both large torcs (collars or necklaces) and a variety of delicate fasteners.

By the 8th century BC Irish smiths were able to create undoubted masterpieces. These included 'lock rings', made with gold wire so thin that the separate threads only show up under a magnifying glass, and the celebrated Gleninsheen gold collar, a crescent filled with regular ribbing and exquisitely hammered raised patterns of threads and circles, with a beautifully crafted disc at each end of the crescent. Irish mastery of these arts was, if anything, enhanced in the final centuries BC, when the island became part of the great Celtic world.

THE DECORATIVE IMPULSE, SO POWERFUL IN EARLY IRELAND, IS APPARENT IN THE FREE, VIGOROUS ZIGZAG PATTERNING CUT OUT OF THIS LINTEL STONE. IT IS PART OF THE MAIN CHAMBER OF A PASSAGE TOMB WHICH STANDS HIGH ON FOURKNOCKS HILL IN COUNTY MEATH

PAGAN CELTIC ART

THE EXISTING TRADITION OF IRISH ART WAS ENLIVENED BY THE MORE FREE-FLOWING, SOPHISTICATED STYLE DEVELOPED BY THE IRON AGE CELTS.

CELTIC, AND PROBABLY CULTIC, THE TUROE STONE (BELOW; FROM COUNTY GALWAY) WAS CARVED AND RAISED FOR PURPOSES THAT REMAIN OBSCURE. ITS SINUOUS LINES AND MOBILE PLANT-LIKE SHAPES HAVE AN INTERESTINGLY MESMERIC EFFECT

Essentially decorative and tending towards abstraction, Celtic art incorporated elements such as spirals and scrolls, tendrils, S-shapes and tiskeles – designs in which three 'legs' issue from a central point, splayed out in a wheel-like fashion to give a strong sense of motion. Rarely symmetrical yet beautifully balanced, Celtic designs were not the result of impulse or wild inspiration: their makers used compasses to create and relate curves and circles, and finds of bone flakes at Lough Crew in County Meath include 'trial pieces' with incised designs, evidently intended as preliminary sketches for works in other media.

In the absence of written records, the history of Celtic art remains full of obscurities. It is often impossible to be sure what function an object was meant to perform, or when, within a time-span of several centuries, it was made. This is especially true of items not associated with a settlement – and many of the finest pieces have been retrieved from bogs and lakes, almost certainly thrown in as part of a religious ritual. Equally mysterious are the 'hoards' unearthed from the ground, notably the gold hoard found at Broighter, County Londonderry, which included a superbly worked collar and a delightful golden model boat; such things may have been ritually buried or simply hidden away for safety.

Many surviving examples of pagan Celtic metalwork are quality pieces, intended for the use or pleasure of chiefs or nobles. Among them is a cache of eight bronze sword scabbards from the River Bann, with all-over decoration in a style that suggests the presence of a school of professional smiths in the area. Long, curved, finely crafted bronze

COMPASS-DRAWN LINES decorate a bone flake from Lough Crew, the site of a Neolithic passage-tomb in County Meath. This and other bone flakes, though found in the actual burial chamber, date from 3,000 years later than the tomb, and their presence suggests that it had a long and continuous history of occupation or ritual use. The flakes were evidently trial pieces, used to work out designs that were intended for use on more valuable materials such as bronze or gold

trumpets from Loughnashade, County Antrim, and Ardbrim, County Down, are likely to have been intended for use on great ceremonial occasions, and it is probably significant that Loughnashade is close to Navan Fort, the site of Emain Macha, the great royal stronghold in the Ulster Cycle. Other bronze objects include a splendid ceremonial headdress, known as the Petrie Crown, and a number of discs with very bold raised designs (two are known to come from Monasterevin, County Kildare); all are reminiscent of the kind of 'Celtic' designs that became fashionable as part of the Art Nouveau style almost two thousand years after they were made.

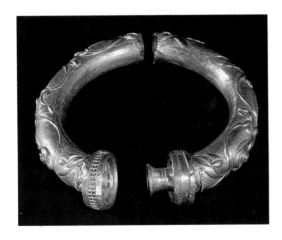

THE BROIGHTER COLLAR IS A GOLD TORC, IN THE FORM OF A HOLLOW TUBE, WITH MAGNIFICENT REPOUSSÉ (BEATEN-OUT) DECORATIONS; IT IS PROBABLY THE FINEST TORC TO HAVE BEEN FOUND ANYWHERE IN THE BRITISH ISLES

Images of humanity – especially the human body – are infrequent in Celtic art. But many small items such as horse trappings (which have survived in surprising quantities) carry designs which can be interpreted as creatures or human heads, often so cunningly concealed that it is sometimes difficult to be sure whether the resemblance is accidental; here we are not far from the shape-shifting of Celtic myth. Further evidence of the Celtic preoccupation with heads (and with the magic number three) is found in the three-faced stone head at Corleck in County Cavan. Celtic designs have not often been found carved into standing stones, and in Ireland only five examples are known from various sites; the most complete is the Turoe Stone (County Galway), a smooth, round-topped granite monument on which the reliefs are particularly elegantly and spaciously set out.

CHRISTIAN FLOWERING

CHRISTIANITY WAS WELL ESTABLISHED IN IRELAND BY THE END OF THE 5TH CENTURY AD, WITH MOMENTOUS CONSEQUENCES FOR THE ARTS.

The Celtic craftsman had to adapt to new subjects and symbols, new objects and media, different patrons and a changed set of underlying values. The principal elements in Celtic design survived the transition, but over time it was much modified by contacts with Germanic and Mediterranean styles, largely thanks to the missionary activities of the Irish themselves; as a result, intricate interlaced ribbons and animal forms were incorporated into designs, along with squares, steps, key patterns and similar figures. The fusion produced a grand new Christian style of extraordinary exuberance, and one which represented the finest flowering of Irish Celtic art.

Among the craftsmen faced by new challenges were the metalworkers, who responded to the demand for liturgical objects, creating examples of church plate which include the famous Ardagh Chalice, a silver vessel whose simple form and plain surfaces are balanced against strips and roundels of intricate filigree decoration in gilt, bronze, gold and enamel, studded with coloured glass and mica. Dating from the early 8th century, the chalice already shows signs of Germanic influence in the animal interlacings on its decorated areas. The new religion also called for representations of the human figure, and here the response was more conservative: despite the change of subject-matter, the figures of the gilt-bronze crucifixion plaque from St John's, Rinnagan, have typically Celtic over-sized heads with schematic features, not much different from those found earlier on pagan deities.

Despite the huge impact of Christianity, the wealthy and powerful continued to delight in personal display. The most impressive surviving objects are brooch-fasteners and buckles and plates on belts, notably the Lagore Buckle and the Tara Brooch. Both roughly contemporary with the Ardagh Chalice, they show another influential Germanic trait, the *horror vacui* or impulse to leave no space, however small, unornamented. This is strikingly apparent on the very

BISHOP ON A HIGH CROSS, WITH TWO ASSISTANTS BENEATH HIM IN THE GRAVEYARD AT KILFENORA, COUNTY CLARE; A CRUCIFIXION IS CARVED ON THE OTHER SIDE. THE MONUMENT IS KNOWN AS THE DOORTY CROSS AND STANDS FOUR METRES HIGH

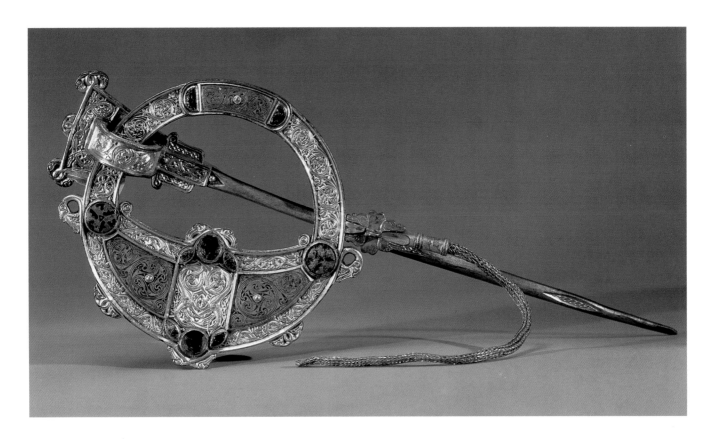

large Tara Brooch (over 22 centimetres long), which is virtually an encyclopaedia of Celtic Irish techniques and decorative motifs. Its royal appearance notwithstanding, the Tara Brooch has no known connection with the seat of the High Kings; it was found in a box on a beach near Bettystown in County Meath.

Christian sculpture in Ireland seems to have begun with crosses carved on to stone slabs in or near early monasteries. By the 7th century masons were carving the stones themselves into crosses; the Cardonagh Cross, County Donegal, is an early example, almost tentative in shape and shallowly engraved. Yet within a century much more assured and impressive 'High Crosses' were being erected, and these became the principal form of monumental art in Christian Ireland. The most obvious factor in their very distinctive appearance is the presence of a circle around the junction of the cross-pieces, which are more or less emphatically indented to create counter-curves. Where a Christ-figure is shown on the cross, these devices serve to frame it, but their origin and significance are still a mystery; plausible but unproved theories identify them variously as solar symbols or wreaths. The tendency towards all-over decoration is strong in the High Crosses, whose relief-work often features bosses and other motifs derived from metalwork; the human figures, though sometimes moving, are still schematic and are often reduced to decorative elements, forming repeat-patterns.

ROYAL JEWELLERY, OR SO IT SEEMS FROM ITS MATERIALS AND WORKMANSHIP. THE WONDERFUL TARA BROOCH IS MADE OF SILVER, GOLD AND COPPER, STUDDED WITH GLASS AND AMBER, AND DECORATED WITH MINIATURE FILIGREE WORK IN THE FORM OF BEASTS AND ABSTRACT PATTERNS

THE ARDAGH CHALICE HAS A MORE SOBER MAGNIFICENCE THAN THE NEAR-CONTEMPORARY TARA BROOCH (ABOVE), PERHAPS IN KEEPING WITH ITS LITURGICAL FUNCTION. THE PLAIN SILVER IS SUPERBLY SET OFF BY AREAS OF INTRICATE FILIGREE

THE ART OF THE BOOK

WITH THE ADVENT OF CHRISTIANITY, BOOKS, READING AND WRITING CAME TO PLAY A SIGNIFICANT PART IN IRISH LIFE. (A FORM OF NOTCH-WRITING, OGHAM, MAY HAVE BEEN USED A LITTLE EARLIER, BUT ONLY FOR VERY LIMITED PURPOSES.)

CELTIC CRUCIFIXION. This gilt-bronze plaque is thought to have been part of the typically elaborate covers made for religious books. Although it dates from the 8th century, the plaque retains some pagan Celtic features, notably the over-large heads. The treatment of the subject is also unusual, with two angels hovering over Christ's outstretched arms and two mourning figures below

Books were precious possessions, since they represented considerable expense and labour: a great number of calf- or sheep-skins were required to make the vellum pages, the entire work was of course hand-written, and duplicates could only be made by copying out the entire text. Furthermore, the intrinsic value of a book was increased when its content concerned the Gospels or some other sacred matter. So it is not surprising that monastic artist-scribes put intense effort into making books that were not merely utilitarian objects but precious works of art.

This was the origin (and not just in Ireland) of the illuminated manuscript: that is, the decorated hand-written book. In its typical form the Celtic illuminated manuscript consisted of pages written in a firm, clear script, with decorative initial letters and borders, occasional 'carpet pages' completely devoted to ornament, and pictures usually intended to illustrate the text; these last, whether large or small, are known as miniatures. A sharpened quill pen was used for writing, and brushes for painting; the pigments, mainly mineral based, included such luxury items such as lapis-lazuli from the East. In Ireland vellum underwent a different processing from its continental counterparts, acquiring a suede texture on which colours stood out boldly. We do not know whether copying and painting were usually done by the same person, but it is clear that long manuscripts were often decorated by more than one artist, sometimes with patently varied results. The finest illuminated manuscripts probably took decades to finish, after which they might be bound in materials incorporating high-quality metalwork and precious stones – which, unfortunately, made them all the more enticing to thieves and, later, to loot-hungry Vikings.

The art of illumination evidently developed slowly. There is very little decoration or colour in the so-called Cathach of St Columba, a copy of

THE EVANGELIST. St Matthew, as portrayed in the Book of Durrow, a 7th-century illumi-nated manuscript of the Gospels. Its beautiful, intricate ornamentation makes a striking contrast to the stiffness of the human figure

the Psalms that is said to have been made by the saint himself, although most scholars believe it was executed some years after his death in 597. One of Columba's foundations, Durrow in County Offaly, has given its name to the Book of Durrow, the earliest substantial Irish illuminated manuscript making extensive use of decoration and colour. Dating from about 675, it contains the Latin (Vulgate) text of the four Gospels, six carpet pages and five other completely illuminated pages including particularly fine renderings of the symbols of the Evangelists. Almost all of the decoration is abstract, but the appearance of biting interlaced animals at one point has led to the belief that the Book of Durrow was made just when Anglo-Saxon influences were beginning to be absorbed, leading on to the illumination style, described as Hiberno-Saxon, that is characteristic of the most celebrated manuscripts.

The Book of Durrow is decorated in a relatively limited range of colours, and its geometric motifs are less crowded and intricate than those of later manuscripts. However, to some tastes its plainness and dignity make it as appealing in its own way as the Lindisfarne Gospels and the Book of Kells.

Despite its name, there is no certainty that the Book of Durrow was actually created at that monastery or even in Ireland; and similar un-certainties hang over other manuscripts, including the Lindisfarne Gospels, the Book of Chad and the Book of Kells. This is because both books and men travelled widely during the great age of Celtic Christianity. Columba and later missionaries carried the skills needed to create illuminated manuscripts to Iona, from there to Scotland and the Northumbrian coast of England, and also across the sea at least as far as Italy. The handful of surviving manuscripts decorated in the Hiberno-Saxon style may therefore have been the work of Irishmen in Ireland, Irishmen abroad, or the pupils of Irishmen anywhere. What is not in question is that the style itself is the creation of Irish monasticism during its golden age.

There is fairly wide agreement that the Lindisfarne Gospels did actually originate on the island of Lindisfarne, off the coast of Northumbria. A celebrated monastery was founded there in 634 by St Aidan, a disciple

A CARPET PAGE FROM THE BOOK OF DURROW. THIS IS THE TERM USED TO DESCRIBE A CROWDED PAGE OF PURE DECORATION; ILLUMINATED MANUSCRIPTS IN THE IRISH TRADITION NORMALLY CONTAINED SEVERAL CARPET PAGES. THE ORNAMENTATION IS NOT ENTIRELY ABSTRACT, THE PRESENCE OF BITING-ANIMAL MOTIFS SUGGESTING SOME GERMANIC INFLUENCE

of Columba, and direct links with Ireland also remained strong: Irish monks are known to have taught on the island, and Eadfrith, bishop of Lindisfarne from 698 to 721, spent six years in Ireland before taking up office. These considerations, backed by other pieces of evidence, make it extremely likely that Eadfrith was both the copyist and the illustrator of the Lindisfarne Gospels.

By contrast, the origins of the damaged and incomplete Book of Chad are a mystery. Although in many respects similar to the Lindisfarne Gospels, it is first recorded in Wales during the late 8th century, reaching its present home (Lichfield Cathedral in the English Midlands) some two centuries later. One obvious possibility is that it was imported into Wales from Ireland, perhaps via the Bristol Channel.

The monastery at Kells (County Meath), though founded by St Columba, was not a great cultural centre, and consequently seems unlikely to have been the first home of the most gloriously lavish and colourful of all the gospel books. But its connection with Kells does seem to have a strong basis in fact. Scholars are increasingly inclined to believe that the manuscript was begun on Iona and then, after Vikings sacked the famous island monastery in 807, carried to Kells by the refugees and finished there. The book may well have been incomplete on arrival, for many of the designs are so intricate that work on it must have taken decades rather than years.

Fine though the Lindisfarne Gospels are, the Book of Kells surpasses them in fluency of line, in colour, and in the sheer inventiveness that enabled the artist (or artists) to decorate a particular letter over and over again without once repeating a design. Even dry reading matter such as the Eusebian Canons, giving long lists of references to parallel passages in the different gospels, becomes a riotous visual feast. But perhaps the most unexpected feature of the Book of Kells is the vein of whimsy and humour that peoples its labyrinthine decoration with unobtrusively placed humans and animals; a celebrated example is the Incarnation Page, with its dominating Chi-rho, the two-letter Greek monogram for Christ, and its mixture of geometric, natural and bizarrely fanciful elements. On occasion even the Celtic reluctance to represent human drama is overcome, as in the scenes of Christ's temptation and his later arrest. Satisfying on many levels, the Book of Kells is one of the world's supreme works of art.

UNSURPASSED for beauty, variety and intricacy of decorative detail, this wonderful page from the Book of Kells is the single most celebrated feature of the work. The text consists of the opening words of the Gospel according to St Matthew, 'Now the birth of Christ. . .' Yet the riot of ornamentation hides a number of images that seem included for purposes of pure amusement: cats and rats, human heads, three angels, and two moths!

A PRECIOUS BOOK. The great Irish illuminated manuscripts were always intended to be seen as precious objects. The result of long and intense labours as well as great skill, exercised to provide worthy versions of sacred texts, such books became treasures with their own aura of holiness, and they were appropriately bound and housed. The small, jewel-studded and intricately carved box holds the Stowe Missal, an Irish mass-book, dating from about 800

THE ARREST OF CHRIST, FROM THE BOOK OF KELLS. A DRAMATIC SCENE
OF THIS KIND IS UNUSUAL IN AN ART FAVOURING ABSTRACT DECORATION AND
THE REPRESENTATION OF FORMALLY POSED SINGLE FIGURES. THE RELATIONSHIP
BETWEEN CAPTORS AND VICTIM IS VIVIDLY CONVEYED

IN THE SERVICE OF THE CHURCH

FROM 795 THE VIKINGS DESCENDED ON IRELAND. MANY MONASTERIES – THE CHIEF CENTRES OF IRISH ART – WERE REPEATEDLY PLUNDERED; COMMUNITIES WERE SLAUGHTERED OR PUT TO FLIGHT, AND UNTOLD QUANTITIES OF FINELY WROUGHT OBJECTS WERE PILLAGED AND ULTIMATELY DESTROYED.

Kells was only one of many monasteries to suffer; its famous book survived, but only after vicissitudes that included a theft in 1006, after which it was buried for three months and retrieved in a sad state, lacking its bejewelled gold cover.

Living traditions are tenacious, and Celtic art survived the Vikings and even absorbed some of the decorative devices employed by their craftsmen. High crosses continued to be carved and standards of metalworking remained impressive during the interval between the Viking defeat at the battle of Clontarf (1014) and the Norman expeditions of the 1170s. The best-known works are reliquaries, containers of various kinds that were made to hold sacred relics such as the bones of saints; because of their special significance they were generally highly wrought and made of precious materials. Often the shape of the container imitated that of the relic inside it. The early 12th-century shrine of St Lachtin's arm is a sturdy and unusual object in the shape of a hand and arm; its wooden base is covered with sheet bronze inlaid with silver and decorated with fascinating wriggling interlaces in a style that owes much to Viking influence.

Other celebrated Irish examples, also from the early 12th century, are the Shrine of St Patrick's Bell and the Cross of Cong. Both reliquaries were commissioned by high kings of Ireland, and the Cross of Cong is highly unusual in carrying the name of the craftsman who made it, the otherwise unknown Maelisu. The Shrine of St Patrick's Bell, one of several surviving bell shrines, is made of bronze, decorated with whorls and interlaces in gold and silver, with large coloured glass bosses. Its wildly extravagant lines of flowing metal give it a mesmerizingly futuristic appearance, while the top in particular has a curiously insectoid look that reappeared in many Art Nouveau objects around 1900.

The Cross of Cong is Ireland's medieval masterpiece, a restrained yet still intense example of the Celtic style. It is made of oak sheathed in silver, with gilt-bronze panels filled with superb interlace patterns; at its centre sits a large crystal, behind which the now vanished relic was installed. Small glass and enamel bosses are set at regular intervals inside the panels and round the contours of the cross. A fierce imaginary animal head bites into the base of the cross from the top of the supporting staff.

STAFF OF OFFICE. THIS FINELY WROUGHT CROSIER WAS MADE FOR NIALL, THE BISHOP OF LISMORE IN COUNTY WATERFORD FROM 1090 TO 1113. THE SHAFT AND CROOK ARE OF BRONZE, FORMERLY GILDED, AND STUDDED WITH GLASS. ONE OF ITS MOST STRIKING FEATURES IS THE ANIMAL-STYLE CREST ALONG THE CURVE OF THE CROOK, INDICATING THE REMARKABLE PERSISTENCE OF ARTISTIC TRADITIONS WITH THEIR ROOTS IN THE PAGAN PAST

Among other ecclesiastical objects from this period are crosiers (bishops' crook-shaped staffs), the best-known being the bronze Lismore crosier. Secular works proved more vulnerable to the chances and changes of time, but in the following period both secular and sacred art were affected by the end of the independent Irish monastic tradition and the arrival of Strongbow and Henry II. A relatively small number of first-class works have survived from the next few centuries, and these are no longer distinctively Irish but in the European style of the time. One example is the Ballylongford Cross, made in 1479 for Cornelius O'Connor, with its delicate, lacelike openwork edging setting off the stark, skeletal figure of Christ, which is very small in relation to the size of the cross. Among the surviving stone sculptures of the period are the 15th-century standing figures in the cloisters of Jerpoint Abbey, County Kilkenny; these vigorously executed carvings of knights, clerics and other medieval types are very different from the idol-like images of earlier Irish sculpture.

THE BALLYLONGFORD CROSS is a fine example of medieval craftsmanship, made in 1479 for Cornelius O'Connor of Kerry. Although highly ornate in late medieval style, this processional cross, its skeletal Christ-figure and its inscriptions on the arms and upper part, owe little or nothing to earlier, specifically Irish artistic traditions. Despite its name, the cross was not found at Ballylongford, but just across the Shannon at Ballycasey in County Clare

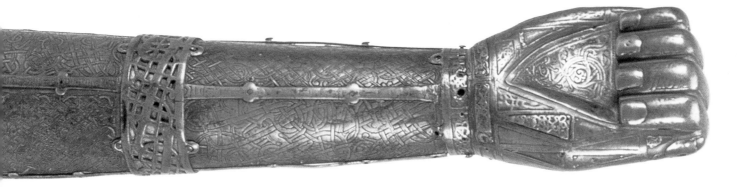

THE SHRINE OF ST LACHTIN'S ARM IS, LIKE MANY OTHER RELIQUARIES, FASHIONED IN THE SHAPE OF THE REMAINS IT WAS DESIGNED TO HOLD; IT IS MADE OF BRONZE INLAID WITH SILVER. DATING FROM ABOUT 1120, IT CARRIES ORNAMENTATION DERIVED FROM THE VIKING URNES STYLE

GEORGIAN ARTISTS

DISTINCTIVELY IRISH ARTISTIC TRADITIONS SEEMED TO
BE IN DECLINE BY THE 15TH CENTURY. BUT THE EVENTS OF
THE FOLLOWING PERIOD SHATTERED THEM FOR GOOD.

The conquest of Ireland by the Tudors led to the imposition of a Protestant state church and the dissolution of the monasteries, while the 17th-century land transfers ruined the other great source of artistic patronage, the chiefs and lords who adhered to Catholicism. New artistic forms were imported from England, including painting in oils and the carving of tomb monuments with realistic effigies of the dead and portrait busts. From the late 17th century, members of the Protestant Ascendancy became the patrons of art, acquiring mainly secular works – portraits, historical set-pieces and landscapes – in the measured, elegant style that established itself over most of northern Europe in the course of the 18th century. In its painting and sculpture, as in its splendid Georgian architecture, Ireland became part of the wider world.

PASTEL PORTRAITS WERE EXTREMELY POPULAR THROUGHOUT THE 18TH CENTURY, PERHAPS REFLECTING THE ERA'S PREFERENCE FOR REFINEMENT RATHER THAN PASSION. THIS SMOOTH, SKILLFUL, GENTLEMANLY PORTRAIT (OF THE SON OF THE ADMIRAL OF THE FLEET) WAS THE WORK OF THE LEADING IRISH PASTELIST, HUGH DOUGLAS HAMILTON

As Ascendancy society grew more sophisticated, painting became a well-established profession, encouraged by the first Irish art school, set up in the 1740s by the Dublin Society and run by the miniaturist Robert West. But although accomplished portraitists such as Garret Morphy (died 1716) and James Latham (1696-1747) worked in their native land, many of the most talented artists inevitably settled in London to pursue their careers. Among them were Charles Jervas (1675-1739), now mainly remembered for his portraits of Jonathan Swift, and James Barry (1741-1806); Barry was regarded as a towering figure in his own day, but his overblown literary-historical set-pieces are now less admired.

By contrast, the best works of the portraitist Nathaniel Hone (1718-84) have worn well, although he is remembered above all for the scandal surrounding *The Conjurer* (1772), which satirized the pretensions of the all-powerful Sir Joshua Reynolds. Unluckily for Hone, the woman artist Angelica Kaufmann believed that she recognized herself in one of the nude figures in *The Conjurer*, and her protests caused the picture to be removed from the Royal Academy exhibition. Hone's outraged response was to put it on show himself, in what is believed to have been the first one-man

exhibition. Hone's son Horace Hone (1756-1825) was a first-rate miniaturist, and Hone's relatives and descendants figure in the history of Irish art right down to the 20th century.

Hugh Douglas Hamilton (1739-1808) established a great reputation in Dublin as a pastelist before he too was drawn first to London and later to Italy. Among artists of a later generation, the miniaturist Adam Buck (1759-1833) and the portraitist Sir Martin Archer Shee (1769-1850) also found fame in England.

The first realistic pictures of Irish life were the works of an Englishman, John Derrick, in the woodcut campaign records of his *Image of Ireland* (1581). More strictly topographical paintings were executed by the early 18th-century Dutch artist Johann van der Hagen, who

SENSE AND SENSIBILITY, restraint and sentiment, are combined in classic Georgian fashion: Lady Louth and her daughter, as portrayed by Adam Buck, might have stepped out of the pages of a novel by Jane Austen

was commissioned to do a series of views of Irish ports. But the finest views of Dublin were by James Malton (d.1803), whose watercolours were published as engravings and quickly became popular classics.

Landscape painting began relatively late, but the variety of the country's scenery and the quality of the light helped to ensure that it became something of a national speciality, attracting many gifted artists in every generation. George Barret (1732-84) was one of the earliest, painting with unusually energetic brushwork and a romantic intensity rarely found so early in the 18th century. Most of his successors worked in a calmer, more classical style; the best-know was William Ashford (1746-1824) who, though Birmingham-born,

AN ARCADIAN LANDSCAPE. THE LEISURED, CULTIVATED LIVES AND COUNTRY HOUSES OF THE 18TH-CENTURY UPPER CLASS FOUND THEIR MOST POETIC MEMORIALIST IN WILLIAM ASHFORD. AS IN ENGLAND, THE GROUNDS OF 'BIG HOUSES' WERE LANDSCAPED TO CREATE AN EFFECT OF NATURALNESS

became the grand old man of Irish art and the first president of the official exhibiting society, the Royal Hibernian Academy, founded in 1823.

Sculpture in the contemporary style was established by two outsiders, John Van Nost (d.1787) and Simon Vierpyl (1725-1810), and their Irish pupils. Edward Smyth (1749-1812) worked under Vierpyl before being employed on Dublin's most celebrated Georgian buildings; he is particularly remembered for his work on the Custom House, which included a series of large, cheerfully grotesque heads representing Irish rivers.

Many British artists visited Ireland, mainly working on portraits and landscapes. During his five years in the country, Francis Wheatley (1747-1801) was unusual in recording official and ceremonial occasions: *View of College Green, with a Meeting of Volunteers, on 4th November, 1779* and *The Irish House of Commons* (1780), pictured at the height of its brief glory as a national senate. Though perhaps not profound, Wheatley was a highly professional and very versatile artist, tackling these and less portentous subjects with a pleasing facility; after returning to England he won enormous popularity with his *Cries of London*.

The 18th century is widely regarded as the supreme age of elegant living: more sociable and decor-conscious than the 17th century, and much less heavy and assertive than the Victorian period which succeeded it. Contemporary ideas of design and decoration were taken up enthusiastically by the propertied classes, who built town and country houses for themselves and filled them with fine furniture, ceramics, silver and glassware; many items were imported, but high-quality objects of true Irish craftsmanship were also acquired, the best-known being the work of Dublin silversmiths and the glass produced at Waterford and Cork. Irish glass-making flourished between 1780 and 1835, initially because the heavy taxes imposed on the industry in England gave Ireland a competitive advantage; the Irish specialized in heavy cut-glass wares, developing a number of distinctive types and exporting to Europe until a change in taste and circumstances depressed the industry. As in painting and sculpture, the applied arts benefited from the presence of foreign craftsmen; this was especially true of plasterwork, one of the staples of 18th-century decoration, which was carried out on a large scale by the Italian brothers Paul and Philip Francini and their many pupils and imitators.

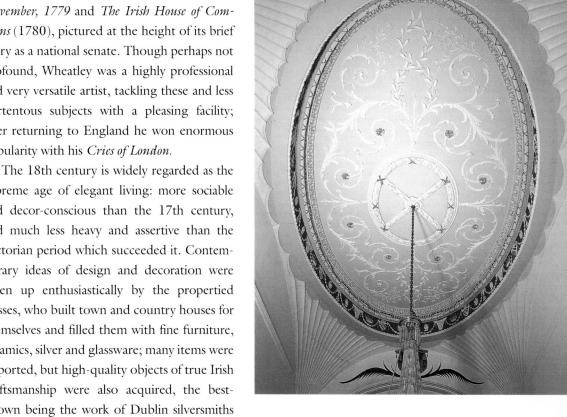

STUCCO HEAVEN: A CEILING AT WESTPORT HOUSE, COUNTY MAYO. PLASTERWORK WAS AN ESSENTIAL 18TH-CENTURY ART, ADDING AN INDISPENSABLE TOUCH OF ELEGANCE TO LARGE INTERIORS; LIKE WEDDING CAKE, IT GAVE AN IMPRESSION OF CHASTE RESTRAINT EVEN WHEN EXTRAVAGANTLY MOULDED

ACADEMICS & IMPRESSIONISTS

IRISH ART FOLLOWED THE PREVAILING BRITISH CONVENTIONS FOR MUCH OF THE 19TH CENTURY, AND IRISH ARTISTS CONTINUED TO GRAVITATE TOWARDS LONDON.

William Mulready (1786-1863) made his name with *The Fight Interrupted* (1816), in which a clergyman separates two boy battlers, and he concentrated thereafter on pleasantly anecdotal paintings, often executed in brilliant, clear colours that have caused him to be regarded as a precursor of the Pre-Raphaelite movement in art. His younger contemporary Daniel Maclise (1806-70) became a history painter and a major figure in the mid-Victorian art establishment. Most famous in his day for patriotic murals in the House of Lords such as *The Death of Nelson* (1865), and able portraits of eminent persons such as his friend Charles Dickens, Maclise applied his talent for large-scale scenes to one key Irish subject, *The Marriage of Strongbow and Aoife* (1854); this huge, tumultuously panoramic view of Norman triumph is, like most history painting of its time, meticulous in detail and yet incorrigibly Victorian in its staging and atmosphere.

THE SPIRIT OF CHIVALRY by Daniel Maclise, an Irish painter who made a career in London and became a friend of Dickens. It represents an idealized view of the Middle Ages, deeply appealing to the Victorians. An Irish harp is prominent in the foreground of the picture

Irish-born sculptors also played their part in creating images of Victorian Britishness. John Henry Foley (1818-74) was the most important of several Irishmen who worked on the Albert Memorial, raised to honour Queen Victoria's husband, which stands in London's Hyde Park. Foley modelled the figure of the prince, cast in bronze, and 'Asia', one of the stone marble groups that surround it.

London promised successful careers to those who could cater to Victorian or imperial sentiments, but some Irish artists were drawn instead to the innovative and often widely abused movements stirring in France. One of the earliest of these artists was Nathaniel Hone the younger (1831-1917), who settled in the 1850s at Barbizon, on the edge of the Forest of Fontainebleau; this was the headquarters of a group of French painters whose fresh, done-from-nature landscapes would lead on to Impressionism.

In France, and later back in Ireland, Hone painted a number of land- and sea-scapes with big skies that were worthy of his mentors. An equally avant-garde figure was Roderic O'Conor (1860-1940). By the time he arrived in Brittany, Impressionism had survived the onslaughts of the critics and the next generation – artists such as Paul Gauguin and

Vincent Van Gogh – were already following new paths. O'Conor became friendly with Gauguin, but stylistically he was more influenced by the strong, thickly applied colours and emotional expressiveness of Van Gogh. A strange, reclusive figure, O'Conor never returned to Ireland. By contrast, another widely travelled artist, Walter Osborne (1859-1903) worked in an Impressionist-influenced version of the academic style to create popular landscapes, city-scenes and portraits.

For all their strengths, 19th-century Irish artists produced very little work that conveyed the distinctive flavour of their native land. That was to change with the arrival on the scene of Jack Butler Yeats.

GIRL MENDING, BY RODERIC O'CONOR, IS THE KIND OF PAINTING THAT GALLERY-GOERS FOUND SHOCKING IN THE LATE 19TH AND EARLY 20TH CENTURIES; THE REASON IS OBVIOUS WHEN ITS COLOURING AND BOLD, LOOSE BRUSHWORK ARE COMPARED WITH THE METICULOUS TECHNIQUE OF VICTORIAN PICTURES SUCH AS MACLISE'S (LEFT)

A CHARMING SCENE BY WALTER OSBORNE. INFLUENCED BY AVANT-GARDE MOVEMENTS SUCH AS IMPRESSIONISM, 'PLAYING ON THE SHINGLE' (1885), THOUGH TRADITIONAL, HAS A BRIGHTER, LESS PORTENTOUS AIR THAN HIGH VICTORIAN PAINTING

INTO THE TWENTIETH CENTURY

THE 'CELTIC REVIVAL' AT THE END OF THE 19TH CENTURY PROMOTED A SENSE OF IRISH DISTINCTIVENESS, BASED ON A RENEWED ENTHUSIASM FOR THE GAELIC LANGUAGE AND 'IRISH SPORTS'.

A mild equivalent in the visual arts was provided by the writer-painter George Russell, also known as AE (1867-1935), but the brightness and charm of his landscapes were often compromised by his technical limitations and rather fey mysticism.

Jack B. Yeats (1871-1957) possessed a stronger and more individual talent, while at the same time projecting a tougher and more down-to-earth image of Irishness. He came from a remarkable Sligo family whose members included his father, John Butler Yeats (1839-1922), a barrister-turned-portraitist, and his brother W. B. Yeats, the famous poet. Much of Jack Yeats's early life was spent in England, but he returned to Ireland in 1900 and developed

OFF THE DONEGAL COAST, a moment of strain and danger captured by Jack B. Yeats in typically energetic fashion. Yeats was a traditionalist in taking his subjects from the older aspects of Irish life, but his expressionistic technique and absence of sentimentality give his paintings an unmistakably individual quality

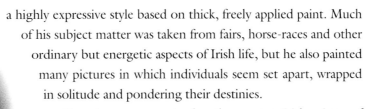

a highly expressive style based on thick, freely applied paint. Much of his subject matter was taken from fairs, horse-races and other ordinary but energetic aspects of Irish life, but he also painted many pictures in which individuals seem set apart, wrapped in solitude and pondering their destinies.

Yeats is now recognized as the greatest Irish painter of the 20th century, but for much of his lifetime the reputations of Sir John Lavery (1856-1941) and Sir William Orpen (1878-1931) stood higher. They became such durable figures in the British art establishment that their Irishness is often ignored. Their careers were curiously similar, culminating in knighthoods for their work as official war artists during the conflict of 1914-18. Both were formidably gifted and painted some good pictures, but failed to achieve the power and profundity of which they had seemed capable; the milieu in which they moved, bringing lucrative commissions for society portraits, has often been blamed, possibly unjustly. Their contemporary Paul Henry (1876-1958) was a more distinctively national artist in taking his subjects from the West of Ireland, although his simplified forms and colours had affinities with British commercial art (book-covers and posters) of the inter-war period.

JACK BUTLER YEATS, PHOTOGRAPHED IN ROGUISH MOOD. YEATS WAS A PROLIFIC AND PROFESSIONAL ARTIST AND WRITER. INDEPENDENT IN STYLE AND ATTITUDE, HE WAS RECOGNIZED AS A GREAT ARTIST ONLY WHEN HE REACHED HIS SEVENTIES

At about this time European modernism was being introduced into Ireland by two closely associated women artists, Mainie Jellett (1896-1943) and Evie Hone (1894-1955). Jellett moved from Cubism to pure abstraction, but Hone became best known for her work in stained glass. This art had undergone a striking revival in Ireland with the foundation in 1903 of the 'Tower of Glass' studio by the painter Sarah Purser (1848-1903) and the emergence of talented stained-glass designers such as Harry Clarke (1890-1931), who managed to produce an impressively large body of work during his short life.

For several decades more, the majority of Irish artists continued to work in semi-academic styles, concentrating on genre, landscape and patriotic subjects. Mirroring Irish society, Irish artists were slow to challenge established institutions. The first breakaway exhibiting society, the Irish Exhibition of Living Art, was not founded until 1943 by Jellett, Hone, Louis Le Brocquy (1916-) and others, long after similar rebellions in most European countries. Later Irish artists responded to the currents and counter-currents of modernity, and the painter William Scott (1913-89) and the sculptor F. E. McWilliam (1909-92) were among those who achieved an international reputation.

SOLIDS AND VOIDS, set off against each other, have become striking features of modern sculpture, in which this preoccupation often leads to dislocations of the human form. In the wood sculpture 'Roman Matron' the Irish artist F.E.McWilliam has made the dislocation all the more striking by carving the individual elements of the figure in a relatively traditional style

FROM TUATH TO TOWN PLAN

LEFT: Custom House Quay; 19th-century view painting
by Claude T. Stanford Moore
RIGHT: High Street, Belfast

STATE ROOMS, Dublin Castle

TOMBS, FORTRESSES AND CASTLES, CHURCHES
AND CATHEDRALS, GEORGIAN TERRACES
AND, VICTORIAN MANSIONS – MUCH OF
IRELAND'S HISTORY IS PRESERVED IN EARTH,
STONE AND BRICK STRUCTURES, ERECTED
FOR PIETY, PROTECTION OR COMFORT

WALLS & RAMPARTS

IRELAND IS A COUNTRY RICH IN ELOQUENT RUINS, NOBLE DWELLINGS AND PLACES DEVOTED TO WAR AND WORSHIP. HER EARLIEST SUBSTANTIAL MONUMENTS ARE THE GREAT PASSAGE TOMBS BUILT IN NEOLITHIC TIMES.

Their main chambers are constructed on a principle that each new generation of children discovers in playing with toy bricks: that two walls of bricks or stones can be piled up, with each level projecting slightly inwards until the tops of the walls are close enough to cap with a final slab. Properly done, this technique (known as corbelling) makes it possible to erect stable structures without using cement (drystone), and Christian monks were still employing it over three thousand years later.

NEOLITHIC TECHNIQUE. A view from below, inside the main chamber of the great passage tomb at Newgrange, County Meath. It shows the method used to construct the five-thousand-year-old roof without any form of cement: large stones are placed one upon the other, slightly overlapping inwards, until the gap at the top is small enough to be covered by a single slab

From about 500 BC, substantial defensive works appeared all over Ireland. This is usually attributed to the warlike character of Celtic society, fragmented into many *tuatha* (kingdoms), although some authorities believe that the largest sites may have served ritual rather than practical purposes. These sites, known as hill-forts, are more or less elaborate systems of stone walls and earth ramparts, following the contours of a hill to create a town-sized defensive structure. It is still not clear to what extent they were ceremonial centres, permanent settlements or simply places of refuge, capable of holding large numbers of people and their herds during a crisis.

Such questions are complicated by the fact that many hill-forts were occupied both before and after the Iron Age; for example, a prominent feature on the Hill of Tara, the so-called Mound of Hostages, is a passage grave. Tara must therefore have a long history as a special place since, long afterwards, during the early centuries of the Christian era, the high kings of Ireland were consecrated there. An equally evocative site, the mound of Navan Fort near Armagh, is the Emain Macha of Irish myth, from which Conchobar ruled Ulster.

Another type of defensive structure was the ring fort. At its simplest, this constituted a farmstead or small settlement surrounded by a drystone wall (cashel) or earth rampart (rath). Many ring forts had souterrains, underground chambers that served as storage-pits or, possibly, hiding-places in the event of the fort being captured. Well-known examples of ring forts are Staigne Fort, County Kerry, and the Grianan of Aileach, County Donegal, both of which have walls up to five metres high, with chambers inside them and steps leading up to the defensive platform at the top.

The crannog was more obviously a place of refuge: a natural or artificial island in the middle of a lake, perhaps linked to the mainland by a hidden causeway. Some crannogs are said to have remained in use until recent centuries, although few traces of them remain. This is certainly not true of the spectacular fortifications on the Aran Islands; although based on the simple principle of fencing off a stretch of territory by building walls from one inaccessible cliff to another, their scale and vertiginous setting are staggering. Dun Aenghus, on Inishmore, boasts three lines of ramparts and, beyond them, a bed of sharp stones, the ancient equivalent of anti-tank defences. In legend, Dun Aenghus was built by an early people, the Fir Bolg, after they were driven from the mainland. Whatever the truth, the evident need to defend these small, bleak islands prompts grim speculations about the quality of life in Celtic Ireland.

SAFE IN THE LAKE. ISLANDS – REAL OR ARTIFICIAL, AS IN THIS LOUGH IN COUNTY ANTRIM – WERE RELATIVELY SAFE PLACES ON WHICH TO SETTLE OR TAKE REFUGE. KNOWN AS CRANNOGS, THEY WERE FREQUENTLY RESORTED TO BY THE CELTIC POPULATION OF IRON AGE IRELAND

HIGH ON A HILL STANDS THE GRIANAN OF AILEACH RING FORT, ON A SITE OCCUPIED FOR MILLENNIA. IT BECAME THE RESIDENCE OF THE O'NEILL KINGS OF ULSTER, WAS STORMED IN 1101, AND AFTER A TURBULENT HISTORY WAS RESTORED IN THE 1870S

EARLY CHRISTIAN LANDMARKS

AT TARA AND EMAIN MACHA, NOTHING REMAINS OF THE ROYAL PALACES AND SETTLEMENTS THAT ARE SAID TO HAVE STOOD ON THESE LARGE, STRATEGICALLY LOCATED SITES.

By contrast, the presence of early Christian communities is felt in many still-quiet places, bearing witness to the impulse of individuals and small groups to seek out remote spots where they could live lives of unworldly asceticism. Some of the more extensive remains also provide direct evidence of the paradoxical fate suffered by some would-be solitaries, whose holiness attracted so many disciples and admirers that the remote spot soon turned into a thriving community.

However, during the early Christian period Ireland's population was small and scattered, and the scale of building and settlement was correspondingly modest. The celebrated monastery on the island of Skellig Michael consists of two oratories (chapels) and six huts in which the monks lived, only big enough to accommodate one or two brothers. The huts are of the 'beehive' or *clochan* type, circular structures made by the same means (with corbelled, unmortared stones) that also served Neolithic builders so well. Founded in the 7th or 8th century on an Atlantic rock and looking down on high, sheer cliffs, Skellig Michael must have seemed the perfect place of self-exile from the world; the monastery was inhabited until the 12th century when, perhaps reflecting altered perspectives within the Irish Church, the community moved to the mainland.

ST KEVIN'S KITCHEN IS AMUSINGLY MIS-NAMED, APPARENTLY BECAUSE ITS BELFRY WAS TAKEN TO BE A CHIMNEY. IT IS ACTUALLY A SMALL ORATORY, ONE OF A CLUSTER OF BUILDINGS IN THE LOVELY VALLEY OF GLENDALOUGH, COUNTY WICKLOW, WHERE ST KEVIN SETTLED IN THE 6TH CENTURY

There are more drystone beehives on the mainland, especially further north on the Dingle Peninsula. But this rudimentary building technique continued in use until quite recent times, and it is often impossible to date examples or even be sure that they were used by monks. The well-known Oratory of Galarus is certainly authentic, but its attribution to the 8th century has been increasingly challenged, and many authorities would now place it much later. This makes all the more striking its small size (6.5 metres in length), still mainly corbelled construction and unusual 'upturned-boat' shape; its sagging roofline has generally been attributed to the unsuitability of corbelling for rectangular structures.

As well as these solitary places, there are many early Christian centres in Ireland which attracted far larger numbers of people and expanded over the centuries. The 6th-century St Kevin retreated to the lovely wooded valley

DRYSTONE HUT, ONE OF MANY ON THE DINGLE PENINSULA, PROBABLY MADE FOR A MONK OR HERMIT BY THE CORBELLING (OVERLAPPING-STONE) TECHNIQUE ALREADY IN USE THREE MILLENNIA EARLIER

of Glendalough in County Wicklow, in search of solitude, but he was not left in peace: even when sleeping on an inaccessible ledge above one of the lakes, he was pursued by an infatuated woman, defending himself ungallantly by throwing her in the water. Less well armed against piety, he acquired so many followers that he ended as the head of a monastery at Glendalough, which henceforth flourished. Later building around the valley's two lakes included an oddly named oratory, St Kevin's Kitchen, St Saviour's Church, a cathedral and many other monuments. After the 16th-century dissolution of the monasteries Glendalough was abandoned, as was the even larger monastery-'city' of Clonmacnoise (County Offaly) founded by St Ciaran in 545, when St Kevin had just begun to occupy his cell at Glendalough. Clonmacnoise was patronized by the kings of Connaught, and churches, workshops and crosses proliferated on the site, which became a great intellectual centre, vigorous despite a long history of attacks and plundering by Vikings and Irish alike.

THE CROSS OF THE SCRIPTURES, one of the most celebrated of Irish High Crosses. These are notable for the distinctive circle that surrounds the junction of the vertical and horizontal members. A Crucifixion and three Passion scenes are carved on the cross, which stands in front of the ruined cathedral at Clonmacnoise

FIGHTING CASTLES

DURING THE 1170S, THE NORMANS MOVED INTO IRELAND AND STEADILY PUSHED BACK THE NATIVE IRISH. THEIR MILITARY SUPERIORITY WAS BASED ON THE QUALITY OF THEIR ARMOURED AND MOUNTED FIGHTING MEN, AND ON THE PART PLAYED IN THEIR CAMPAIGNS BY CASTLES.

As developed by the Normans, the castle was a multi-purpose instrument of war and government. It provided a stronghold in which a lord and his men could sleep safely in a hostile land, and a place of refuge if

TRIM CASTLE, the largest Anglo-Norman fortress in Ireland. Despite its size, its origin is obscure and its defensive strength questionable. Trim is believed to have been built early in the 13th century. Its outer wall, defended by D-shaped towers, is efficient enough, but the huge keep had four attached towers, creating a number of weak points

their enemies gained the upper hand. But a castle might also function as a forward post in a general advance, securing fresh territory, deterring local resistance, and serving as a base for reconnoitering and a further advance against the enemy. Finally, when the countryside was pacified, it was a highly visible symbol of dominance, leaving no one in doubt about who was master.

THE BROKEN WALLS OF DUNDRUM, ON THE COAST OF COUNTY DOWN. THEY NO LONGER FORM A FIRST LINE OF DEFENCE FOR THE CIRCULAR KEEP, A FEATURE THAT WAS ONCE THE LATEST REFINEMENT IN 13TH-CENTURY MILITARY TECHNOLOGY

The Normans believed so strongly in the value of castles that they put up temporary structures as quickly as possible. (They had done the same in England after 1066.) Unskilled local labour could be used to throw up a ditch-encircled mound of earth and stone (the motte), on which a timber tower and palisade were raised; if this was linked with a secondary, ground-level enclosure (the bailey), the result was the well-known motte-and-bailey type of castle.

Many of the mottes can still be identified, but the timber towers vanished long ago. By about 1200 some lords were already building in stone, raising great rectangular keeps (towers) with first-floor living quarters where the lord and his family could try to sit out a siege; the keep was the place of last resort, the front line of defence being the strong wall around it, all the more effective if it was reinforced at intervals by wall-towers from which crossfire could be directed against the enemy. The castle of Carrickfergus (County Antrim) was built on this pattern in the early 1200s, while the biggest of all Norman-Irish castles, at Trim (County Meath), was completed a few decades later, in time to incorporate more up-to-date ideas in the form of wall-towers with round outer faces, less vulnerable than corners to undermining activities. A circular keep was built, for the same reason and probably at about the same time, at the spectacularly sited Dundrum (County Down).

SPLENDIDLY PRESERVED, Carrickfergus Castle stands on a rocky spur above Belfast Lough. It has a large square keep and two surrounding curtain walls. Begun late in the 12th century, it was captured by King John in 1210 and served intermittently for centuries as a royal castle. Carrickfergus last saw action in 1760, when it was briefly occupied by French raiders

After this, castle-construction followed the prevailing English style, with powerful gatehouses, portcullises, barbicans, machicolations and other sophistications. Royal castles were most technically advanced, dispensing with keeps and relying on mighty walls with strong round towers (each of which was in effect a keep) to guard and overawe towns such as Dublin, Limerick and Roscommon. The early advantage held by the invaders waned as the native Irish learned how to build in Anglo-Norman fashion – quite directly in the case of Ballintober, erected by the O'Conors of Connaught at the end of the 13th century, after they had twice captured, occupied, studied and eventually destroyed nearby Roscommon Castle.

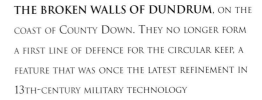

THE AGE OF FAITH

THE WARLIKE HABITS OF THE VIKINGS CREATED MANY OF IRELAND'S FINEST RUINS, BUT TRACES OF BUILDINGS PUT UP BY THE VIKINGS THEMSELVES ARE VIRTUALLY NON-EXISTENT OUTSIDE MUSEUMS AND HERITAGE CENTRES.

THE ROCK OF CASHEL, APPROACHED FROM ANY DIRECTION, OFFERS THE VISITOR ONE OF IRELAND'S MOST FASCINATING SKYLINES. THIS VIEW FROM THE NORTH SHOWS THE SEPARATE ROUND TOWER WITH THE SQUARE CENTRAL TOWER OF THE CATHEDRAL BEHIND IT

By contrast, the Irish continued to erect monasteries and churches, although conditions were uncertain enough for them also to put up a tall round tower on most important ecclesiastical sites from the 9th century onwards; the sixty-odd surviving examples include towers at Glendalough, Clonmacnoise, the Rock of Cashel and Ardmore (County Waterford). There has been some debate about their function, and is likely that they served in peaceful times as bell towers. But their importance as places of refuge is shown by the fact that, unlike other monastic buildings, they were not drystone structures but set with mortar.

Moreover their entrances, like those of castle keeps, were on the first floor; the fleeing inhabitants reached the entrance by a ladder which they could draw up behind them, enabling them to sit out the most common, hit-and-run type of plundering raid.

In the 12th century the European Romanesque style reached Ireland, and buildings began to display such characteristic features as round arches and vaulting, arcading, sculptures above doors (in the tympanum, between the arch and the lintel) and decorative motifs such as the chevron. But Irish ecclesiastical buildings remained small, and the common church plan consisted of a simple rectangle (the nave) with a narrower rectangle added at one end as the chancel (the part of the church exclusive to the clergy).

Ireland's earliest Romanesque church, Cormac's Chapel, has a slightly more elaborate version of this plan, with a tower set in on each side of the building where the nave meets the chancel. The carvings of humans and real and imaginary creatures is in the Romanesque style, treated with a certain extra Irish quirkiness, and the traces of fresco painting found in the chapel are the earliest known in Ireland.

Cormac's Chapel was begun in 1127 and completed in 1134 by Cormac McCarthy, who combined political and spiritual power in his

A SYMBOL OF TROUBLED TIMES, a tall round tower was erected on many religious sites, providing a place of refuge from Viking and other marauders. The fine example at Ardmore, on the south coast was built as late as the 12th century

own person as king of Desmond and bishop of Cashel; a sarcophagus in the chapel is said to be his tomb. The chapel itself stands on one of the most romantic sites in Ireland, the Rock of Cashel, high above the town of Cashel in what is now County Tipperary. When the chapel was built, the other important monument on the Rock was the 24-metre-high, 11th-century round tower, which still stands there in excellent condition, complete with its conical cap. The round tower is still an imposing sight, but Cormac's Chapel is dominated by the sheer bulk of the 13th-century cathedral, whose roofless ruins have given a fortuitous air of 'Gothick' mystery to the skyline of the Rock.

The cathedral on the Rock of Cashel was built after the Anglo-Norman conquest of Ireland. The way in which it dwarfs Cormac's Chapel indicates the larger, 'European' scale on which the newcomers conducted their affairs. However, influences from outside had begun to reach the Irish Church some thirty years before the conquest, fired by St Malachy's determination to reform – and make uniform – its organization and customs. The reformers began in 1142 with the foundation of Mellifont (County Louth), the first Cistercian abbey in Ireland. Daughter abbeys were rapidly established with the help of imported master masons; among the most interesting, in their present condition, are Jerpoint (County Kilkenny) and Ballintubber (County Mayo). As a result of the 16th-century Reformation and the dissolution of the monasteries, all of these foundations survive only as ruins, but they are moving sights as well as often preserving carvings and other features of historical and aesthetic interest.

POIGNANT REMAINS. The ruins of Mellifont Abbey are reminders of Ireland's past religious conflicts. As the first Cistercian abbey in Ireland, it may well have been viewed as a foreign intruder; by the 16th century it was one of many well-loved monasteries that fell victim to the innovating religious policies of the English crown

A century after the dissolution of the monasteries, a great number of Irish ecclesiastical buildings were damaged or vandalized by iconoclastic Cromwellian soldiery, who often made a point of stabling their horses in churches and cathedrals. But unlike most monastic buildings, churches were useful in the new Protestant dispensation, and consequently a number of medieval foundations were taken over and remained in use down to the 20th century.

This has inevitably meant that most were altered or rebuilt over the centuries. Dublin has no fewer than two cathedrals, both founded in the 12th century, but thanks to restorations and rebuildings they are more Victorian than anything else, though filled with details of historical interest. Christ Church Cathedral is the oldest building in Dublin, erected

ROMANESQUE SCULPTURE. ROMANESQUE WAS THE GREAT EUROPEAN STYLE OF THE EARLY MIDDLE AGES, LATER SUPPLANTED BY GOTHIC. THE 12TH-CENTURY DOORWAY AT CLONFERT CATHEDRAL EXEMPLIFIES ITS GROTESQUE AND FANTASTIC ELEMENTS, INCLUDING THE ANCIENT MOTIF OF BITING ANIMALS

from 1172 with the powerful support of Strongbow, the first of the great Anglo-Norman lords to carve out a fiefdom for himself in Ireland. Its great rival, St Patrick's Cathedral, was built only half a kilometre to the south, so that it stood outside the jurisdiction of the existing cathedral. It was begun in 1191, one of the prime movers being a certain Henri de Londres, who was at least partly motivated by his disputes with the Christ Church authorities. In time St Patrick's became the largest church in Ireland; both it and Christ Church were taken over by the Protestant Church of Ireland, and even today there is no Roman Catholic Cathedral in the capital of the Republic. Despite the impetus to building given by the Normans, only a very small number of Irish cathedrals and churches are medieval in origin. Fewer still retain an authentic medieval character; among the best examples are the Cathedral of St Canice at Kilkenny and the Church of St Multose, Kinsale.

ST PATRICK'S CATHEDRAL IN DUBLIN, BELIEVED TO HAVE BEEN THE SITE OF CONVERSIONS EFFECTED BY ST PATRICK HIMSELF. ST PATRICK'S IS FILLED WITH MANY INTERESTING MEMORIALS, INCLUDING THE GRAVE OF THE GREAT WRITER JONATHAN SWIFT

FROM TOWER HOUSE TO MANSION

WARFARE AND PLAGUE HELPED TO MAKE THE 14TH CEN-
TURY A PERIOD WHEN RELATIVELY LITTLE NEW BUILDING
WAS DONE. BUT DURING THE 15TH CENTURY THERE WAS
AN UPSURGE OF ACTIVITY IN WHICH MANY ABBEYS AND
OTHER ECCLESIASTICAL BUILDINGS WERE REMODELLED
OR EXTENDED.

The most striking secular development was the construction of tower
houses all over the country. The trend began early in the 15th century
and continued until about 1650, so that such towers are the commonest
of all pre-modern structures in the Irish landscape. Essentially the tower
house is a small-scale castle keep – a usually rectangular tower, most
often four or five room-sized storeys high, large enough to house a family and its servants with dignity if not in comfort. There might also be
one or more smaller towers or turrets at the corners to hold the stairs
and extra chambers. Dunsoghly (County Dublin) is a tower house with
four such 'flankers' and, uniquely, its original
medieval roof. The tower stood within a walled
enclosure, or bawn; most of these have since
disappeared (their walls plundered for building
stone), but good examples survive at Dungory
(County Galway), Knockelly (County Tipperary) and Rathmacknee (County Wexford).
Tower houses were also put up in towns; the
most fascinating is at Clonmines (County Wexford), where not only the tower but the entire
town is ruinous, having been abandoned in the
17th century when sand choked its harbour.

The very existence of so many tower houses
is evidence that life in Ireland remained
extremely insecure; a similar development
occurred in England during the 14th and 15th
centuries, but whereas comfortable, unfortified
residences became normal during the Tudor
period, Irish lords and gentry (and English and
Scottish newcomers) found it prudent to live
in cramped but strongly defended quarters for
a further century and a half. Since this was a
period of conquest, plantation, rebellion and
civil war, the persistence of tower-house building scarcely requires an explanation. There
were nevertheless signs that the balance
between security and comfort was beginning
to tilt towards comfort. An early but excep-
tional example is the mansion at Carrick-
on-Suir (County Tipperary), built up against

A TUDOR MANOR HOUSE, PUT UP IN A
STILL-UNTAMED IRELAND. THE EARL OF ORMONDE'S
MANSION AT CARRICK-ON-SUIR, COUNTY TIPPERARY,
DATES FROM 1580 AND ANTICIPATES NOT ONLY THE
CONQUEST OF IRELAND BY THE ENGLISH CROWN BUT
ALSO THE TRANSITION FROM GRIM, UNCOMFORTABLE
FORTRESSES TO PLEASANT, MANY-WINDOWED ABODES,
EQUIPPED WITH THE LATEST AMENITIES. AT CARRICK
THE CHANGEOVER IS MADE VISIBLE IN MASONRY,
SINCE THE HOUSE WAS BUILT BY THE EARL DIRECTLY
ON TO THE 15TH-CENTURY CASTLE INHERITED FROM
HIS FOREBEARS

the 15th-century castle; it is still a remarkable and rather disconcerting sight. The mansion, an unfortified Tudor manor house dating from the 1580s, perhaps expressed the lordly confidence of its builder, the Earl of Ormonde, the head of the powerful Butler family.

Much more common were mansions that allowed for greater comfort but retained some defensive features. These include two early-17th-century 'castles', the never-finished Kanturk (County Cork), whose formidable air is contradicted by the ranges of windows (letting in both light and enemies), and Portumna (County Galway), a large and splendid Jacobean mansion whose defences consist of little more than firing holes around the main entrance. When the upheavals of the 17th century seemed at last to have subsided, new, elegant and unfortified residences such as Beaulieu (County Louth) began to appear in the 1660s and, despite the interruption of King William's war, heralded an age of fine public and domestic building.

A SAFE PLACE. Standing on a promontory in Galway Bay, Dunguaire Castle was built in the 16th century, like Carrick (opposite), but represents a more pessimistic view of general security. Though called a castle, it is really a tower house, a smaller, less expensive residence that was designed to protect its occupants against hit-and-run raiding parties rather than withstand a full-scale siege

DUBLIN'S FAIR CITY

IN GAELIC, DUBLIN IS 'BAILE ATHA CLIATH' (TOWN OF THE HURDLE FORD) OR 'DUBH LIN' (THE DARK POOL), BOTH VERY ANCIENT NAMES.

Nevertheless the city's real founders were the Vikings; their first settlement (841) was short-lived, but under the intriguingly named Ivar the Boneless they founded a city-state in 917 that endured until the Anglo-Normans arrived in 1170.

The fortunes of medieval Dublin waxed and waned along with those of the English royal authorities, although the city was always important because of its position as a port and its administrative role as the capital of the Pale. Christ Church and St Patrick's Cathedral and Dublin Castle all date from its first Anglo-Norman phase, and the renewed expansion under the Tudors led to the building of another great Dublin landmark, Trinity College; founded in 1592 by Queen Elizabeth I, who graciously described it as being 'for the reformation of the barbarism of this rude people', Trinity College was in reality meant to offer an Irish Protestant alternative to the foreign and Catholic universities where many Irishmen studied.

The modern history of Dublin begins after the Restoration of the exiled Charles II in 1660 and the return to Ireland of James, Duke of Ormonde, as the viceroy. Like other exiles, Ormonde brought back a new awareness of Continental arts and fashions, and during his long rule (1662-85) a more sophisticated Dublin began to emerge. The city began to spread rapidly beyond the medieval walls, and speculative builders created new developments such as St Stephen's Green. Many Dutch-style houses were built, their gable-ends facing the street, and the Royal Hospital, Kilmainham (1680), designed by Sir William Robinson, became the first Irish public institution to be constructed in the classical style.

A few years of renewed uncertainties ended with William III's victory in 1690 at the battle of the Boyne and the subsequent triumph of the Ascendancy. Dublin now became more prosperous than ever, as service industries grew up to supply the grandees who built town houses or flitted between viceregal Dublin Castle and an increasingly important Irish parliament. Huguenot (French Protestant) refugees from persecution

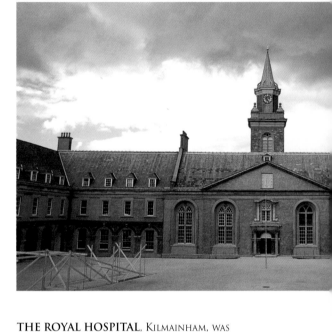

THE ROYAL HOSPITAL, KILMAINHAM, WAS IRELAND'S FIRST GREAT CLASSICAL BUILDING, BEGUN IN 1680 TO A DESIGN BY THE IRISH SURVEYOR-GENERAL, SIR WILLIAM ROBINSON. RUNNING ROUND ALL FOUR SIDES OF A COURTYARD, IT WAS MODELLED ON LES INVALIDES IN PARIS

GEORGIAN DUBLIN is famous for its great public buildings, and also for fine terraces of private houses, mostly plain and discreet but often subtly varied in the interests of individuality. The doorways display interesting variations on mock-architectural features such as columns, arches and pediments. The 'peacock-tail' fanlights above many doors are much admired

brought in superior craft skills, and English and Continental artists and architects were now glad to work, and sometimes settle, in Ireland. In the course of the 18th century, Dublin became the second city of the British Empire, behind London in terms of population and wealth, though not in beauty and amenities.

Some fine buildings date from the early 18th century. Marsh's Library (1702) and Trinity College Library (1712) are particularly notable for their atmospheric interiors. Tailors' Hall (1706), formerly a guild hall, is a fine plain brick building of the Queen Anne period which now houses Ireland's National Trust; and the imposing Dr Steeven's Hospital (1720) was the first private hospital in the country. Then began the surge of building that would transform Dublin into a great Georgian-classical city.

The enhanced importance of Dublin, and of the country's Ascendancy élite, was signalled by the building of a meeting-place for the Irish Parliament. Time has turned this into 'the Old Parliament House', now the headquarters of the Bank of Ireland, but it was the first building since Antiquity to be specially

LIT BY A HUNDRED WINDOWS, THE INTERIOR OF TRINTY COLLEGE LIBRARY IS A BIBLIOPHILE'S DREAM THROUGHOUT ITS 82-METRE, BARREL-VAULTED LENGTH – EXCEPT, PERHAPS, FOR THE DISTRACTION FROM THE PRINTED PAGE THREATENED BY ITS VISUAL SPLENDOUR. LIKE THE BRITISH LIBRARY, IT RECEIVES A COPY OF EVERY BOOK PUBLISHED IN THE BRITISH ISLES

constructed for a representative assembly. It was begun in 1729 to designs by Edward Lovett Pearce (d.1733), a talented Irishman working in a period when the really big commissions generally went to British and Continental architects. Pearce's work ensured that the dominant style for at least a generation would be Palladianism, a version of ancient Roman architecture, with its porticos, pediments and colonnades, based on the work of the Renaissance Italian architect Andrea Palladio (1508-80); as imported into Britain by Lord Burlington (1694-1753), Palladianism became synonymous with the kind of patrician grandeur to which the aristocracy and gentry of Britain and Ireland alike aspired.

Pearce's early death meant that the group of splendid town houses built in the wake of the Old Parliament House in the 1730s and 1740s were the work of his assistant, the German-born Richard Cassels (or Castle; c.1690-1751); in that cosmopolitan age, Cassels seems to have had no difficulty in adapting to Irish taste. His designs, all for Palladian buildings dressed with Portland Stone, included Clanwilliam House on St Stephen's Green (1738; now part of Newman House), Tyrone House

TRINITY COLLEGE, Dublin, is Ireland's premier university, its famous graduates ranging from Jonathan Swift to Samuel Beckett. The view across Parliament Square shows the 18th-century Dining Hall (left) and the Victorian Graduates' Memorial Building

(1741) and Leinster House (1745), and also a maternity hospital in similar style, the Rotunda (1748). Built for the powerful Earl of Kildare (later Duke of Leinster), Leinster House is the largest of Cassels' town houses, a palace-like mansion of such dimensions that since 1921 it has been the seat of the Parliament of the Irish state.

The elegances and amenities of Dublin were greatly improved during this period, which saw the shaping into its present form of Phoenix Park

THE CUSTOM HOUSE, DESIGNED BY JAMES GANDON, AN ENGLISH ARCHITECT BROUGHT TO IRELAND BY HIS PATRON LORD CHARLEMONT. CONTROVERSIAL IN ITS OWN DAY, IT IS NOW REGARDED AS AN UNQUESTIONABLE MASTERPIECE

THE FOUR COURTS, Dublin, Gandon's other masterpiece on the north bank of the Liffey. This majestic building survived shelling by government forces during the 1922 civil war, although 700 years of irreplaceable public records were destroyed by the ensuing fire. The colonnaded gallery beneath the dome offers fine views of the city

(the largest public gardens in Europe); the remodelling of Dublin Castle; the re-making of much of Trinity College including its imposing west front; and excellent town planning supervised by the Commissioners for Making Wide and Convenient Streets, a body whose creation in 1757 was one of the most enlightened acts of the Irish Parliament. Though aristocratic town residences such as Sir William Chambers' Charlemont House (1762) continued to be built of stone, brick was used in the construction of new streets and squares, whose agreeable variety is exemplified by Merrion Square (laid out from 1762).

Ireland attracted a number of English architects, including Thomas Cooley (designer of the Royal Exchange, now City Hall, Dublin) and the better-known Sir William Chambers (1723-96), whose delightful Casino, a small temple-pleasure-house at Marino, Dublin, is arguably his finest achievement. But it was Chambers' pupil, James Gandon (1743-1823), brought over to Dublin in 1781, who set the seal on the Georgian city, creating two masterly public buildings, the Custom House (1781-91) and the Four Courts (1785-1802), in a superb setting on the north bank of the Liffey.

THE BIG HOUSE

THE SURGE OF WEALTH AND CONFIDENCE THAT CREATED GEORGIAN DUBLIN WAS ALSO RESPONSIBLE FOR THE BUILDING OF LARGE COUNTRY HOUSES AND FINE BUT MORE MODEST DWELLINGS ALL OVER RURAL IRELAND.

As in England, the aristocratic 'big house' displayed both the wealth and the good taste of its owners, combining arcadian settings with sophisticated elegance, hosts of servants, and every available comfort. The house generally stood in extensive parkland (in Ireland called the demesne) which was traversed by long drives and given touches of light-hearted fantasy in the form of mock-temples, obelisks or statuary.

Palladianism and other variations on classical ideals determined the outward appearance of the big houses, while the interiors were opulent, whether decorated in the frothy curvilinear Rococo style or the more stately Neo-classical style that displaced it. The paintings that hung there reinforced the impression of untroubled harmony, contradicted in many places by the continuing but unrepresented misery of the peasantry. Nevertheless it was not a matter of pure snobbery when the poet W. B. Yeats mourned the passing of the traditional loveliness symbolized by a big house such as the now-vanished Coole Park, home of his patron-friend Lady Augusta Gregory, where so much of value to the Gaelic and literary revival was planned and executed.

Although many have disappeared or have been gutted, the 18th-century big houses still exist in substantial numbers. The largest and grandest, Castletown in County Wicklow, was also one of the earliest. It was built from 1722 for William Connolly, a shrewd entrepreneur who ended as Speaker of the Irish House of Commons. The architect, Alessandro Galilei (1691-1737), had an unusual itinerary. Born in Florence, he emigrated to England, failed to find appropriate work there, and so moved on to Ireland. Despite his success at Castletown and elsewhere, he returned to Italy, where his most important commission was to design a new façade for a famous early Christian church in Rome, St John Lateran. Meanwhile for his assistant, Pearce, working at Castletown (where he had been responsible for the internal designs) marked the real beginning of his short career.

The subsequent wave of country-house building coincided with the Dublin boom, and many of the same busy architects were involved. Pearce designed Bellamont Forest (County Cavan) in 1729-30, and Cassels' wide practice included Westport (Mayo), Carton, not far from Castletown (in an area boasting many big houses), and the now burned-

STATELY HOME THE ENTRANCE HALL TO WESTPORT HOUSE IN COUNTY MAYO EPITOMIZES THE SPACIOUS, GRACIOUS SETTINGS IN WHICH THE ANGLO-IRISH ARISTOCRACY DWELT. THE STAIRCASE IN WHITE SICILIAN MARBLE LEADS TO THE PRINCIPAL ROOMS ON THE FIRST FLOOR. THE HOUSE WAS DESIGNED BY RICHARD CASSELS IN 1730 AND EXTENDED HALF A CENTURY LATER BY THOMAS IVORY AND JAMES WYATT

GRANDEST OF ALL. Ireland's largest Palladian house, Castletown in County Wicklow, was built for a self-made man, William Connolly, and was intended from the first to be a showpiece, 'the finest Ireland ever saw and. . . fit for a prince'. The building consists of a central block, with splendid curved colonnades sweeping away on either side. A different kind of 18th-century taste appears in two follies and other features in the grounds

NOBLE RUIN. POWERSCOURT HOUSE MIGHT STAND AS A SYMBOL OF THE TRADITIONAL LOVELINESS WHOSE PASSING WAS LAMENTED BY THE IRISH POET W.B.YEATS, HOWEVER, POWERSCOURT WAS NOT A VICTIM OF THE TROUBLES OF THE 1920s, BUT WAS GUTTED BY FIRE IN 1974. TO DATE, ALL PROJECTS FOR ITS RESTORATION HAVE FOUNDERED IN THE FACE OF THE ENORMOUS EXPENSE INVOLVED. HOWEVER, THE LOVELY GARDENS ARE OPEN TO ALL

out but still impressive Powerscourt House in County Wicklow. Sir William Chambers and two other well-known British architects, James Wyatt and John Nash, also worked in Ireland; among Wyatt's designs were interiors at Powerscourt House and its model village. Many good houses were the work of lesser-known Irish builders such as Isaac and John Rothery and the Johnston brothers. More talented than these was another little-known figure, the Sardinian Davis Ducart, architect of Kilshannig (Cork) and the lovely Castletown Cox (Kilkenny) which, though relatively small, can stand comparison with any house in the land.

THE VICTORIANS

IRELAND IS RICH IN BUILDINGS, IN VARIOUS STATES OF PRESERVATION AND DATING FROM WIDELY DIFFERENT PERIODS; MEMORIALS OF DIVERSE CULTURES, CLASSES AND CONVICTIONS OFTEN STAND CLOSE TOGETHER, UNITED AT LEAST IN DEFYING TIME.

In the present day, the type of building most under threat is one that many people see as quintessentially Irish – not the big house or even the church or monastery, but the whitewashed and thatched cabin, evocative

ANCIENT AND MODERN. KILLYLEAGH CASTLE, SOUTH-EAST OF BELFAST, HAS A TURBULENT PAST, BUT MOST OF THE PRESENT BUILDING IS A VICTORIAN FANTASY – A 'CHÂTEAU' CRAMMED WITH WINDOWS

of the simple life and Gaelic speech. Even in its last western strongholds, those who have to live in such cabins have understandably rejected romance and opted for alterations or rebuilding in the interests of convenience and comfort.

The towns and villages of Ireland have also changed, but fortunately the best elements of the past have often been preserved. Urban life began in the Viking era, but the modern history of towns really dates from the 16th century. Derry is an early example of a planned settlement, reflecting its origin as a Protestant stronghold, laid out during the 17th-century plantation of Ulster; it still boasts a complete circuit of the walls that kept out King James's followers. But many more towns and villages were planned or improved in the following century, and still have their original courthouses and markets – and also the ubiquitous barracks which show the 18th-century order in a rather different light.

In the number of its Georgian survivals the city of Armagh is second only to Dublin, but in a less concentrated form the Georgian heritage can be found everywhere, from the Bishop's Palace at Waterford to the spacious model town created by the Earl of Kingston at Mitchelstown (County Cork) and the endearing village houses curving round the green at Tyrelspass in Westmeath.

ST STEPHEN'S GREEN is one of the most popular places in Dublin, although many of its fine Georgian houses have been demolished. The green, Sir Arthur Guinness's bequest to the public in the 1870s, is still a superb city park, filled with walks, flower-beds, fountains, bandstands, statues and an ornamental pond

The Georgian tradition (and the Georges) persisted into the 19th century, but in Ireland, as elsewhere, architectural styles gradually took on the imposing but heavier aspect of Victorianism. Victorian architecture was once deplored – and, more reasonably, its makers were condemned for confidently tearing down so many fine buildings from earlier periods; but the solid virtues of the best Victorian works are now widely recognized. Dublin was spared the worst excesses of rebuilding as an indirect result of the 1801 Act of Union. After the abolition of the Irish Parliament, the Ascendancy grandees were drawn away from Dublin to the new centre of power at Westminster. Heavily dependent on aristocratic patronage, Dublin's economy was seriously damaged, and so there was relatively little new building – or tearing down of the old – in the heart of the city. Not all the results were a conservationist's dream, however, since areas north of the Liffey, including once-elegant Georgian terraces, went into terminal decline and turned into some of the worst slums in Europe. At the same time, an expanding middle class took advantage of the new railway and tram systems to move out into

GEORGIAN ARMAGH. A TERRACE OF FINE HOUSES IN THIS NORTHERN CITY BEARS WITNESS TO THE ENDURING INFLUENCE OF THE 18TH CENTURY, MORE WIDELY DIFFUSED IN IRELAND THAN ALMOST ANYWHERE ELSE

the suburbs, which spread out rapidly towards Howth in one direction and Killiney in the other.

One of the paradoxes of the Victorian period (1837-1901) was that magnificent, visionary feats of engineering went hand in hand with architectural styles that were entirely derivative. Revivalism ran riot, as architects ransacked their pattern-books, turning from Classical to Gothic, and from Gothic to Romanesque, Renaissance, Baroque and even 'Neo-Egyptian' modes. In Ireland, the Gothic style was frequently used for Church of Ireland buildings, and that may have encouraged Catholic authorities to remain faithful to the Classical style when an ambitious construction programme began in the more tolerant atmosphere of the 1820s; the Pro-Cathedral in Dublin is of special interest as an excellent example of the severe and scholarly Greek Revival style, all the more intriguing since its designer is unknown.

Apart from familiar types of domestic dwelling, the Victorians created a large number of mercantile and institutional buildings, including libraries, museums and galleries, asylums and prisons, banks, offices and railway stations. They were also prolific designers of public houses (bars), sometimes of such a baroque and inventive nature as to give a new slant to the notion of 'Victorianism' and reinforce the already pronounced predilections of the citizenry. In its various aspects Victorianism modified the character of Georgian Dublin and Limerick, and effectively created present-day Belfast and Cork.

Victorian revivalism also influenced the building of country houses, which might take the form of Scottish baronial or Elizabethan edifices, complete with billiard rooms and all other modern conveniences. Nostalgia for the Middle Ages expressed itself in the construction of castles – or rather, of mansions with battlements and other sham-medieval features. Most were not intended to serve any serious military function, but the architect E. W. Godwin did assure his client, the far-from-popular Earl of Limerick, that the mighty walls of his new castle at Dromore would protect him in the event of a Fenian rising.

In the event, the 20th century proved far more destructive. The Easter Rising, the Troubles, the Blitz and the ambitions of corporations and developers have all taken their toll. Nevertheless the architectural heritage of Ireland remains one of her greatest attractions.

VICTORIAN STRONGHOLD. Belfast Castle stands on the slopes of Cave Hill, on the outskirts of the city overlooking Belfast Lough. It was built as a suitable residence for the Marquess of Donegal in the late 1860s by W.H.Lynn. The style, typical of 19th-century revivalism, is 'Scottish Baronial', inspired by the mock-baronial pile built at Balmoral for Queen Victoria and Prince Albert. Typical features are the cone-capped towers, the bartizans (towers perched halfway up the building) and the 'crow-stepped' gables

A **REMOTE PALACE** IN THE HEART OF CONNEMARA, KYLEMORE CASTLE WAS CREATED AT ENORMOUS EXPENSE FOR THE BRITISH MILLIONAIRE MITCHELL HENRY. FINISHED IN 1862, IT CONTAINED 70 ROOMS. DURING THE FIRST WORLD WAR IT PASSED TO NUNS WHO HAD FLED FROM THEIR OWN CONVENT AT YPRES, WHEN IT ACQUIRED ITS PRESENT NAME, KYLEMORE ABBEY

SACKVILLE STREET, DUBLIN'S MAIN THOROUGHFARE (PRESENT-DAY O'CONNELL STREET), IN THE EARLY 19TH CENTURY. THE MOST PROMINENT FEATURES ARE THE GENERAL POST OFFICE, FLYING THE UNION JACK, AND THE NELSON PILLAR. THE GPO BECAME THE HEADQUARTERS OF THE EASTER RISING

AN ELOQUENT PEOPLE

LEFT: The Cliffs of Moher, County Clare
RIGHT: The poet W.B. Yeats

THE LAKE OF INNISFREE on Lough Gill, County Silgo

FAMOUS THROUGHOUT THE WORLD FOR
WIT AND GOOD TALK, THE IRISH HAVE ALSO
EXERCISED THEIR VERBAL GIFTS ON PAPER.
THEIR WRITINGS IN ENGLISH HAVE MADE
AN IMPRESSIVE CONTRIBUTION TO
WORLD LITERATURE

THE GAELIC HERITAGE

CENTURIES BEFORE THE INTRODUCTION OF WRITING,
THE CELTS OF IRELAND WERE COMPOSING STORIES AND
POEMS IN GAELIC THAT WERE COMMITTED TO MEMORY
AND PASSED DOWN FROM GENERATION TO GENERATION.

The earliest script, known as Ogham, was used on monuments of stone, and was evidently developed through contacts with Roman Britain, since it was based on twenty letters of the Roman alphabet and is believed to have been current from the 3rd century AD. Each letter was represented by a series of notches along or across the edge of the stone, giving the inscription a code-like appearance.

Ogham was the earliest Irish writing, but it was not literature: the stones merely record a man's name and his family. The first Irish literature was written by monks from the 5th or 6th century who copied and composed not only in Latin but in Gaelic; their achievement,

MYSTERIOUS ALPHABET. THE GROUPS OF LINES CUT INTO THIS WELL-WORN STANDING STONE IN COUNTY KERRY ARE OGHAMS, LETTERS OF AN ALPHABET THAT WAS USED FOR THE FIRST IRISH WRITING IN THE EARLY CENTURIES

still not widely realized, was to create the first vernacular literature in Europe. Thanks to them, the great cycles of Irish myths have survived, along with many poems, stories and reflections that were composed by the monks themselves.

The professional poets attached to the courts of kings and chiefs rapidly became literate and began to set down their own works and the traditions – especially the elaborate genealogies – which it was their task to preserve. These poets were either *fili* or, less aristocratic and less steeped in ancient lore, bards; but both are now commonly referred to as bards. As well as preserving the memory of great men and great deeds of the past, the bard was expected to write 'praise-poems' that would raise his master to a similarly heroic level. Such bardic verse, produced in vast quantities, was notable for its skill in handling well-worn themes and its extraordinary intricacy.

Bards wrote for an aristocratic audience, and the collapse of the old Gaelic order in the 17th century doomed them; with their patrons dispossessed, they became impoverished and often ended as proud, embittered vagabonds. Gaelic poetry continued to be written for a popular audience, often by poor 'hedge' schoolmasters whose classes were held out of doors. In the 18th century, the aisling, or vision-poem, expressed the hope against hope that the exiled Stuarts would come again and liberate Ireland.

Gaelic was still widely spoken in 1800, although English was already the language of the cities and of all who aspired to office or influence. The spread of elementary education (in English) and the effects of the Famine, which struck hardest in Gaelic-speaking areas, turned a decline into a disaster. Gaelic seemed about to die out, but the foundation of the Gaelic League (1893), and the work of Douglas Hyde (1860-1949) in particular, re-created interest in the language and sponsored new writing in it. The Irish Free State put its authority behind the revival, and many fine Gaelic works have been published. But despite the official status of Gaelic, English remains the first language of most Irish people, and that situation seems unlikely to change. Since Irish attachment to Gaelic remains very strong, the Republic seems certain to be bilingual for the foreseeable future.

WRITING IN IRISH. STUDIOUS MONKS ADAPTED THE ROMAN ALPHABET TO IRISH SPEECH AND CREATED THE FIRST WRITTEN GAELIC LITERATURE. AMONG OTHER THINGS THEY RECORDED THE GREAT MYTHICAL CYCLES IN WORKS SUCH AS 'FELIRE OENGUSO', OF WHICH A MANUSCRIPT PAGE (PROBABLY A 12TH-CENTURY COPY) IS SHOWN BELOW. IN DOING SO, THE MONKS ALSO CREATED THE FIRST POST-ROMAN VERNACULAR LITERATURE IN EUROPE

A MEMORIAL. This Ogham stone is one of nine at Ballintaggart on the Dingle Peninsula. Most of the few surviving Oghamic inscriptions have been found in southern Ireland and South Wales; their basis in the Latin alphabet indicates the strength of Roman influence on even those Celts who remained outside the Empire

THE DEAN OF ST PATRICK'S

KNOWN THROUGHOUT THE WORLD AS THE AUTHOR OF GULLIVER'S TRAVELS, JONATHAN SWIFT WAS A FEROCIOUS SATIRIST, A MAN OF DISAPPOINTED AMBITIONS, AND ONE OF THE MORE UNLIKELY IRISH NATIONAL HEROES.

Swift was the son of an English lawyer who died before his birth in Dublin on 30 November 1667. Educated at Kilkenny School and Trinity College, Dublin, he was a wayward student, granted his BA in 1686 by 'special grace'. In 1689 he became the private secretary to the retired diplomat Sir William Temple, and lived at Temple's house, Moor Park, in Surrey until 1699, apart from a short period in which he was ordained and worked as an Anglican priest in Ireland. At some point during these years he met a young woman, Esther Johnson ('Stella'), with whom he formed an intimacy whose precise nature remains obscure.

When Temple died, Swift returned to Ireland, where he received a living and a prebend in St Patrick's Cathedral, Dublin; Stella and her companion, Rachel Dingley, joined him there but never lived with him. Often in England, Swift published a number of satires and political pamphlets which eventually won him the patronage of the Tory ministry. His activities are described in the letters to Esther Johnson, which were published after his death as the *Journal to Stella*; but at the same time he formed an equally enigmatic relationship with Esther Vanhomrig (the 'Vanessa' of his poem *Cadenus and Vanessa*). In 1713 Swift was appointed Dean of St Patrick's, Dublin, but the succession of George I and the triumph of the Whigs ended all hope of further preferment. He returned to Dublin in 1715, comparing himself to 'a poisoned rat in a hole'.

Despite his often unflattering remarks about Ireland, Swift used his literary gifts in her interests. In 1720 he proposed that the Irish should retaliate against British trade barriers by consuming only home products: 'Burn everything English but their coal.' In 1724 his *Drapier's Letters* inspired the successful Irish opposition to 'Wood's Halfpence' (page 56). He became a popular hero, and when he returned to Dublin in 1726 after a visit to England, flags

JONATHAN SWIFT, in one of many portraits by Irish artist Charles Jervas. Avoiding the ornate and tortuous, Swift perfected the plain style of English prose, achieving a clarity and force that made his satiric thrusts unanswerable. Had his ecclesiastical ambitions been more successful, he might not have served Ireland so well

Captain *Lemuel Gulliver, of*
Redriff Ætat. suæ 58.

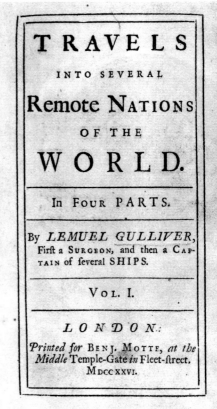

TRAVELS

INTO SEVERAL

Remote Nations

OF THE

WORLD.

In FOUR PARTS.

By *LEMUEL GULLIVER*,
Firſt a SURGEON, and then a CAP-
TAIN of ſeveral SHIPS.

VOL. I.

LONDON:
Printed for BENJ. MOTTE, *at the*
Middle Temple-Gate *in* Fleet-ſtreet.
MDCCXXVI.

MAN AMONG MANNIKINS. GULLIVER'S
TRAVELS IS A FEROCIOUS COMMENTARY ON HUMAN
PRETENSIONS AND THE CORRUPTION OF 18TH-CENTURY
SOCIETY. BUT SWIFT'S CONCEPTION OF GULLIVER AS
A MAN AMONG TINY LILLIPUTIANS HAS MADE THE
STORY, IN SIMPLIFIED FORM, A CHILDREN'S CLASSIC

were put out, bells rung and bonfires lit. In 1729 he became a freeman of Dublin while publishing his *Modest Proposal*, satirizing the kind of economic 'realism' that takes no account of moral or human values: since the people were so poor and numerous, Swift argued, the logical course was to raise, fatten and sell Irish children like cattle, for their meat.

Meanwhile, in 1726 Swift had published the immortal *Gulliver's Travels*. As a brilliantly ingenious parable of contemporary corruption and human pretensions in general, *Gulliver* won immediate popularity, although its scourging of human failings reaches an almost unbearable climax of loathing in the episode where Gulliver lives among the noble horse-people, the Houyhnhnms, beside whom his own kind, the Yahoos, are revealed in all their vileness; on his return to England he finds even his own family disgusting. The evolution of Swift's satire into a children's story – taken from the episode in Lilliput – is one of the curiosities of literature.

In the 1730s Swift's health was increasingly undermined by an affliction, now believed to have been Ménière's disease, which caused giddiness and nausea. He became insane in March 1742 and died in 1745; according to his epitaph in St Patrick's, he had gone 'where fierce indignation can no longer tear the heart'.

THE TRUE TITLE. PROPERLY SPEAKING, THERE IS NO SUCH TITLE AS 'GULLIVER'S TRAVELS'; HOWEVER, IT IS A VERY CONVENIENT ABBREVIATION, AS CAN BE SEEN FROM THE TITLE PAGE OF THE FIRST EDITION, SHOWN ABOVE. SWIFT'S BOOK FIRST APPEARED IN 1726, COMPLETE WITH A PORTRAIT OF ITS SUPPOSED AUTHOR, LEMUEL GULLIVER

PLAYWRIGHTS
& PHILOSOPHERS

ALTHOUGH SWIFT SPENT MUCH OF HIS LATER LIFE IN DUBLIN, MOST 18TH-CENTURY IRISHMEN WHO HOPED TO MAKE A LIVING BY THE PEN HEADED FOR ENGLAND; THE ONLY OTHER DISTINGUISHED EXCEPTION WAS THE PHILOSOPHER GEORGE BERKELEY, BISHOP OF CLOYNE.

Berkeley is remembered for his theory of perception which helped to undermine the common-sense, cause-and-effect theories of the time. The series of gifted Irishmen who sought fame and fortune in London made a quite extraordinary contribution to English life and literature. Without exception, these writers graduated from Trinity College, Dublin, before adopting the precarious existence of a professional writer; and most of them were more anxious to be accepted as English gentlemen than literary geniuses. This was as true of William Congreve (1670-1720),

ALL IS REVEALED! IN SHERIDAN'S COMEDY THE SCHOOL FOR SCANDAL, SIR PETER TEAZLE AND CHARLES SURFACE FLING DOWN A SCREEN, EXPECTING TO ENJOY THE EMBARRASSMENT OF A PRETTY FRENCH MILLINER, HIDDEN BY CHARLES'S BROTHER. INSTEAD, SURFACE AND TEAZILE FIND THEMSELVES LOOKING AT A MORTIFIED LADY TEAZLE

who was born in Yorkshire but brought up in Ireland, as of the Dubliner Sir Richard Steele (1672-1729). Steele collaborated with Joseph Addison in writing for *The Spectator* (1711-12), and in so doing established the modern essay in its urbane, whimsical, mildly didactic mode; Congreve wrote comedies of manners such as *The Way of the World* (1700) which have arguably never been surpassed for lightness of touch, wit and acuteness of characterization.

Meanwhile the theatre in Dublin, though deserted by the most talented writers, managed to flourish. The first playhouse in the city opened in 1635, but was soon shut down by the Cromwellian prohibitions which also interrupted the English theatrical tradition. After the Restoration of Charles II in 1660, the first Dublin theatre to open was Smock Alley, which achieved a certain eminence in the 1740s and '50s under Thomas Sheridan (1719-88), who managed to attract leading performers such as David Garrick for his sparkling 1744-5 season. However, Dublin's day as an outstanding theatrical centre was still to come.

One writer who did work at Smock Alley (as an actor) until he left for London was George Farquhar (1677-1707); towards the end of his short life he wrote two rollicking minor classics, *The Recruiting Officer* (1706) and *The Beaux' Stratagem* (1707). Sentimental comedies were popular for much of the 18th century, until works by two Irish writers led to a reaction. *She Stoops to Conquer* (1773) by Oliver Goldsmith, and *The Rivals* (1775) and *The School for Scandal* (1777) by Richard Brinsley Sheridan, have held the stage ever since their early performances, although they now seem far from abrasive. Goldsmith (c.1730-74) was notable as an essayist and a novelist (*The Vicar of Wakefield*), and his poem *The Deserted Village*, a minor classic with many frequently quoted lines, contains a number of reminiscences of his own Irish home at Lissoy. Richard Brinsley Sheridan (1751-1816), the son of the manager of Smock Lane, was a writer, Member of Parliament and proprietor of the Drury Lane Theatre. His fame as an orator has been eclipsed by that of his fellow-Irishman Edmund Burke (1729-97), whose career as a leading Whig politician was ultimately less important than his writings as an aesthetic theorist and, in *Reflections on the French Revolution* (1790), the chief philosophic advocate of social and political conservatism.

DESERTED VILLAGE. 'THE SAD HISTORIAN OF THE PENSIVE PLAIN', A CURIOUSLY WILD FIGMENT OF THE ENGRAVER'S IMAGINATION, LISTENS TO THE LAST INHABITANT OF THE VILLAGE IN THIS VIGNETTE ACCOMPANYING OLIVER GOLDSMITH'S LONG POEM. THE POEM IN FACT FEATURES NO HISTORIAN EXCEPT GOLDSMITH, NOSTALGIC FOR HIS VILLAGE CHILDHOOD

THE MISTAKES OF A NIGHT IS THE APPOSITE SUB-TITLE OF GOLDSMITH'S COMEDY SHE STOOPS TO CONQUER. BELIEVING HE IS AT AN INN, THE NORMALLY BASHFUL MARLOW MAKES LOVE TO THE YOUNG LADY OF THE HOUSE, WHOM HE TAKES FOR A SERVANT. THE TWO FATHERS OF THE COUPLE EAVESDROP, BEMUSED BY THE UNEXPECTED TURN OF EVENTS

IRELAND IN STORY & SONG

DURING THE 19TH CENTURY, IRISH WRITERS CONTINUED TO SEEK THEIR FORTUNES IN ENGLAND; BUT UNLIKE THEIR 18TH-CENTURY PREDECESSORS, THEY VERY OFTEN WROTE ABOUT THEIR NATIVE LAND.

This reflected a change in public taste brought about by the Romantic movement and Sir Walter Scott's novels of Scottish history, which created a vogue for the local and regional, especially where they were associated with a stirring 'primitive' past. But as Scott himself acknowledged, it was not he but the Irish writer Maria Edgeworth (1767-1849) who produced the first regional novel, *Castle Rackrent* (1800). Pithy, comic and painful, Edgeworth's story packs a wealth of incident and observation into a small space, chronicling the decline of the wilful, reckless Rackrent family, as witnessed over three generations by their loyal steward, Thady Quirk; after the final smash-up, it is Thady's calculating lawyer son who emerges as the new owner of the castle.

CROCODILE TEARS from Judy M'Quirk, when the feckless Sir Condy talks of his imminent demise; he is only self-dramatizing, but his prediction will be realized sooner than he expects. The illustration from Maria Edgeworth's 'Castle Rackrent' captures the disorder, false hopes and sham emotions accompanying self-ruin

The poet Thomas Moore (1779-1834) exploited the new taste in more sentimental fashion, publishing no less than ten volumes of *Irish Melodies* (1808-34). His nostalgic verses, set to traditional melodies, enjoyed an enormous popularity, rivalled only by his *Lalla Rookh* (1817), which was based on an alternative form of Romantic escapism, into luxuriant Orientalism. During his lifetime Moore was second only to his friend Lord Byron in poetic renown; he has since been undeservedly neglected, and few people are even aware that he is the author of *The Last Rose of Summer* and other minor classics.

More sinister subjects preoccupied several other Irish writers. Charles Maturin (1780-1824) created one of the more extravagant 'Gothick' novels of terror, *Melmoth the Wanderer* (1820). More sophisticated effects were achieved by Joseph Sheridan Le Fanu (1814-73), a novelist and journalist who found his true vein late in life. *Uncle Silas* (1864) makes the plight of the heroine, an heiress surrounded by murderous relatives, almost unbearably frightening and claustrophobic; whereas *In a Glass Darkly* (1872) displays Le Fanu's skill as a teller of supernatural stories. His tale *Carmilla*, about the depredations of a female vampire, influenced another Irish-born author, Bram Stoker (1847-1912), when he came to write *Dracula* (1897).

DOMESTIC CHAOS. A COMIC INTERLUDE IN LE FANU'S HISTORICAL NOVEL COLONEL TORLOUGH O'BRIEN. DICK GOSLIN IS HIDING IN A CAULDRON WHEN TWO SERVANT GIRLS POUR A TUB OF COLD WATER INTO IT. HE LEAPS OUT, IMPALING THE TUB ON HIS HEAD, THE MAIDS TAKE FRIGHT, AND CHAOS ENSUES

George Moore (1853-1933) introduced the realism of the 19th-century French novel to English literature. His most celebrated work, *Esther Waters* (1894), describes the tribulations of an English working-class girl, but Moore later became an important figure in the Irish literary revival and was instrumental in the planning of the Irish National Theatre. The twilight of Anglo-Irish society, often evoked in 20th-century writing, was described at first hand in *The Real Charlotte* (1894) and other novels by 'Somerville and Ross' (the second cousins Edith Somerville, 1858-1949, and Violet Martin, 1862-1915). But their most popular works were the comic tales in *Some Experiences of an Irish R. M.* (1899) and its sequels, in which the English resident magistrate, Major Yeates, suffers one ludicrous disaster after another at the hands of the wiley Irish over whom he is supposedly in authority; though dependent on stock types, the situations are handled with a deft, light touch that makes them quite irresistible.

STAGE IRISHMEN

DURING THE MIDDLE DECADES OF THE 19TH CENTURY
THE ENGLISH-LANGUAGE THEATRE WAS QUITE UNDISTIN-
GUISHED, BUT IT DID PRODUCE ONE COLOURFUL AND
ENERGETIC FIGURE IN DION BOUCICAULT (1820-90), AN
IRISH PLAYWRIGHT AND ACTOR-MANAGER WHO ENJOYED
EQUAL SUCCESS IN BRITAIN AND THE UNITED STATES.

After making his name with the drawing-room comedy *London
Assurance* (1841), Boucicault wrote or adapted over 150 plays. *The
Colleen Bawn* (1860) and *The Shaughraun* (1874) presented the Irish
character in a singularly attractive if somewhat sentimental light, but
most of Boucicault's output consisted of melodramas with sensational
heroine-on-the-railway-line climaxes.

Boucicault's work lost favour when a more
naturalistic drama established itself, but Irish
fantasy and artifice triumphed in the plays and
stories of Oscar Wilde (1854-1900). Wilde's
personal history has become more widely
known than his writings, ironically validating
his claim that 'I have put my genius into my
life, and only my talent into my art.' After a brilliant university career, he
began a course of ardent self-promotion, appearing in 'aesthetic' velvet
breeches, delivering carefully honed epigrams, and publicly adoring celebrated actresses. Though he lecture-toured
America in 1882, Wilde's poetry and other
writings brought in little money and, having
married, he took on the editorship of *Woman's
World* magazine (1887). His fairy tales and
essays demonstrated that a substantial talent
lay behind the public persona, and in the
1890s it came to fruition with the epigram-
studded novel *The Picture of Dorian Grey*
(1891), three problem-dramas lightened by
superbly witty passages, and *The Importance of
Being Earnest* (1895), which transforms the
English social scene into an absurd never-never
land. In 1895, at the height of his fame,
Wilde's involvement with Lord Alfred Douglas
drew him into a disastrous libel action, made
public his homosexuality, and led to his trial
and imprisonment. After his release he spent
his last years, self-exiled, in France.

JOHN BULL'S *OTHER ISLAND* neatly describes
Ireland under British rule. Bernard Shaw's comedy with
that title was highly successful, thanks to the British
enjoyment of satire directed against themselves. In 1911
a special command performance (above) was given at
The prime minister's residence 10 Downing Street

A SLIGHT DISAGREEMENT, pictured in the
frontispiece of *Used Up*, the published version
of a comedy by Dion Boucicault. The element of
melodrama is typical of Boucicault, who was very
in tune with the tastes of 19th-century audiences

Thanks to his longevity, Bernard Shaw (1856-1950) seems a far more
modern figure than his near-contemporary Wilde. Born into a Dublin
family with pretensions but little money, Shaw worked for five years as a
clerk before coming to London in 1876. After years of failure writing

unpublished novels, he gradually made his way as a critic, producing writings on music and the drama that are classics of lucidity, humour and polemical vigour. Meanwhile he had become a pillar of the socialist Fabian Society, and his earliest plays, *Widowers' Houses* (1892) and *Mrs Warren's Profession* (1898), were exposés of contemporary injustices.

Over the following half-century Shaw created a dazzling one-man theatre of ideas, filled with witty dialogue and situations, and a strong sense of fun that sometimes went over into farce. Among his best-known plays are *Arms and the Man* (1894), *Man and Superman* (1905), *Pygmalion* (1913), *Heartbreak House* (1919) and *St Joan* (1923). Shaw was indisputably a master of prose (in criticism, play-prefaces and letters), and although his plays have become unfashionable during periods that cherish anguish and ambiguity, their durability hardly seems in question.

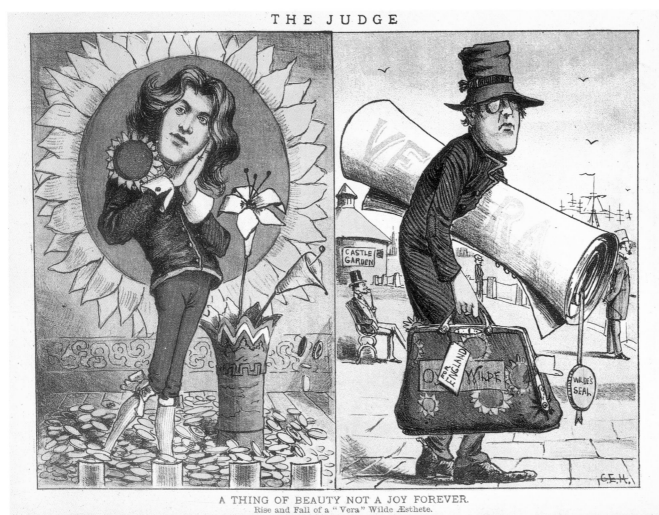

THE JUDGE

A THING OF BEAUTY NOT A JOY FOREVER.
Rise and Fall of a " Vera " Wilde Æsthete.

FRAGILE CELEBRITY. In his youth, Oscar Wilde promoted himself as an aesthete in silk breeches, boasting of his exquisite sensibility and genius. The amusement of public and press alike was tinged with a puritanical irritation that surfaces in this gloating commentary on the failure of Wilde's play Vera. His subsequent writings won him fame and wealth, but his terrible fall was greeted with moralistic wrath mixed with jubilation

THE MASTER POET

WILLIAM BUTLER YEATS (1865-1939) IS OFTEN THOUGHT OF AS AN ALMOST SYMBOLIC FIGURE – THE QUINTESSENTIAL IRISH POET, A WRITER OF HIGH SERIOUSNESS CLOSELY IDENTIFIED WITH THE NATIONAL CAUSE.

Of Anglo-Irish stock, Yeats in fact spent much of his boyhood in England, and returned there for very long periods until quite late in life. However, during school holidays in Sligo he absorbed the Irish legends and folklore that would always haunt him. At the end of three years at the School of Art in Dublin (1884-7) he emerged as a poet and an advocate of national revival, but also as a dedicated student of the occult, which provided many of the ideas underlying his work.

Yeats's first verse collection, *The Wanderings of Oisin* (1889), made him a leading figure in the nascent 'Irish revival', and one of his most popular poems, 'The Lake Isle of Innisfree', appeared soon afterwards. The 'Celtic Twilight' mood of his work was also in tune with much British writing of the 'decadent' '90s, and Yeats spent much of his time in London, where he was a member of the Rhymers' Club and had an early play, *The Land of Heart's Desire*, performed on the stage in 1894 alongside Bernard Shaw's *Arms and the Man*.

Yeats's involvement with the stage deepened after his meeting with Lady Gregory in 1896, and he made an immeasurable contribution, literary and practical, to the flowering of Irish drama and the establishment of the Abbey Theatre

W.B.YEATS in later life, 'a public smiling man' who had served a six-year stint as a Senator of the Free State. Yeats proved a surprisingly successful and pragmatic lobbyist for the causes he supported, whether the staging of a play threatened by censorship or the return to Ireland of paintings whose ownership was disputed by the National Galleries of London and Dublin. His last poems and plays were as intensely felt as ever, lamenting old age, celebrating sexuality, and attempting to penetrate beyond the veil of human existence

(page 142). During this period he experienced a long-lasting, unrequited love for Maude Gonne, a beautiful, fiery apostle of Irish nationalism. When Yeats's *Cathleen ni Houlihan* was performed in 1902 she took the title part – symbolic of Ireland – but in 1903 she married John MacBride, a man of action rather than a poet. Yeats himself was never able to embrace wholeheartedly the rhetorical simplicities of nationalism. Even the famous poem 'Easter 1916' is ambivalent in its admiration for the 'terrible beauty' created by men whose act of timeless heroism transcends their mortal frailties. For Yeats, such an escape from mediocrity and time was also provided by

IRELAND HERSELF VISITS A HUMBLE COTTAGE, SEEKING 'LOVERS' WHO WILL FIGHT TO FREE HER, IN YEATS'S PLAY CATHLEEN NI HOULIHAN, SHOWN IN PHOTOGRAPHS OF THE FIRST PERFORMANCE IN 1903. MAUDE GONNE, WHOM YEATS LOVED HOPELESSLY FOR YEARS, PLAYED CATHLEEN, SYMBOL OF IRELAND

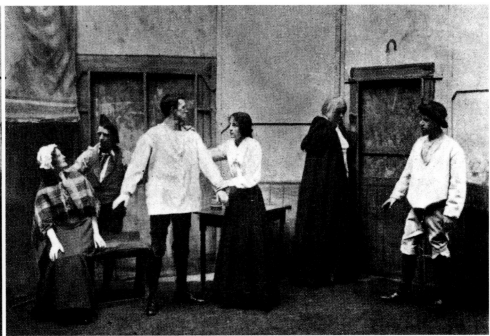

TOWER HOUSE HOME. THOOR BALLYLEE WAS PURCHASED BY YEATS IN 1919 AS A SUMMER HOME IN COUNTY GALWAY, NOT FAR FROM THE COOLE PARK ESTATE OF HIS FRIEND LADY GREGORY. THE TOWER FEATURES IN YEATS'S POETRY AS A SYMBOL OF TRADITIONAL ORDER OR, WHEN FALLEN, ITS PASSING

art, as described in, and exemplified by, his famous poem *Byzantium*.

Yeats developed continuously as a poet, abandoning the 'Celtic twilight' manner of his youth for a sparer vocabulary and more precise images. Ultimately he developed a unique style that was as direct and simple as natural speech yet intensely charged with meaning and emotion.

In 1917 he married George Hyde-Lees, whose mediumistic 'automatic writing' led to the creation of the poet's own hermetic system, described in *A Vision* (1926). From the 1920s Yeats made Ireland his permanent home; he served as a senator (1922-8) and was awarded the Nobel Prize for Literature (1923). He was prolific as a poet and playwright until his death, writing of art and mystery, raging against old age, elegizing the passing of time and destruction of beauty, and enjoying a variety of personae without ever ceasing to be completely himself.

THE LITERARY REVIVAL

DURING THE LATE 19TH CENTURY, IRISH NATIONALIST FEELING TOOK CULTURAL AS WELL AS POLITICAL FORMS. THE GAELIC ATHLETIC ASSOCIATION PROMOTED 'IRISH SPORTS', A NATIONAL LITERARY SOCIETY WAS FOUNDED IN 1892, AND AT ITS INAUGURAL MEETING DOUGLAS HYDE SPOKE ON 'THE NECESSITY FOR DE-ANGLICIZING IRELAND'.

SPREADING THE NEWS IS THE TITLE OF THE PLAY, AND IS EXACTLY WHAT SEEMS TO BE GOING ON IN THIS PRODUCTION BY THE ABBEY THEATRE. IT IS A RUSTIC COMEDY WRITTEN BY AN ANGLO-IRISH ARISTOCRAT, LADY AUGUSTA GREGORY, WHO WAS TO BECOME ONE OF THE FOUNDERS OF THE IRISH NATIONAL THEATRE

Hyde went on to become the president of the Gaelic League, dedicated to the revival of the Irish language; but interest in old Irish ways, peasant life and folklore also led to the development of a literature in English that captured their essential flavour with creative em- pathy and lively new idioms.

Translations and retellings of stories and legends began as early as the 1860s, but popular interest became stronger from about the time that W.B.Yeats published *Fairy and Folk Tales of the Irish Peasantry* (1888) and *The Celtic Twilight* (1893). In 1896 Yeats encountered a young man named Synge in Paris, and advised him that the traditional way of life on the grey, remote Aran Islands would provide him with original literary material. And in the same year Yeats met an aristocratic widow,

Lady Augusta Gregory, and the two plotted to create a theatre that would be dedicated to Irish plays on Irish subjects.

The Irish Literary Theatre was founded in 1899 by Yeats, Lady Gregory, the lesser-known writer Edward Martyn, and the novelist George Moore. By 1902 the Irish National Theatre Society, a talented company led by Frank and W. G. Fay, was performing plays by Yeats and the writer-artist George Russell (AE). In 1904 the Society was able to take over disused premises on Abbey Street, Dublin, and the famous Abbey Theatre was born. Yeats and Lady Gregory became long-serving directors and also provided much of the company's repertoire; the opening night consisted of three one-acters, *Cathleen ni Houlihan* and *On Baile's Strand* by Yeats, and Gregory's comedy *Spreading the News*.

A key figure in the literary revival, Lady Gregory (1852-1932) began her career as a dramatist late in life, through her connection with the National Theatre Society; she wrote over forty accomplished pieces, most of them short peasant comedies. An Anglo-Irish aristocrat who entertained a wide literary circle on her Coole Park estate, she developed strong nationalist sympathies but defended writers impartially against popular prejudice and government censorship. The most celebrated Abbey controversy was the near-riot provoked in 1907 by Synge's *Playboy of the Western World*. John Millington Synge (1871-1909) had taken Yeats's advice and paid annual visits to the Aran Islands, soberly described in a book published in 1907. The experience sharpened his ear for native idioms and rhythms, which he adapted and fashioned into a style all of his own. *The Playboy* is the best-known of the handful of plays he wrote during a life cut short by Hodgkin's disease; its poetic dialogue, and the rollicking amorality which outraged its earliest audience, have long since made it a classic.

The Abbey Theatre's creative role in Irish life was recognized in 1925 when it was officially subsidized. By no means tamed, it staged the plays of Sean O'Casey (1880-1964), whose slum settings and questioning of patriotic values were deeply upsetting experiences for Irish audiences.

J.M.SYNGE, author of *The Playboy of the Western World* and other plays inspired by the way of life (and echoing the speech) of the far west of Ireland. The portrait above is by John Butler Yeats, whose poet son (W.B.Yeats) suggested to Synge that the Aran Islands would yield a rich new vein of literary material; and Synge's subsequent visits to the islands did in fact give his writing a direction it had previously lacked

PLAYBOY TRIUMPHANT. Christy Mahon, the hero of Synge's *Playboy of the Western World*, is accepted as the husband-to-be of Pegeen Mike. In this 1921 production at London's Royal Court Theatre, Pegeen is played by Maire O'Neill, the love of Synge's final years, who created the part at the Abbey Theatre, Dublin, in 1907. The performances during the first week were interrupted by protesters with trumpets, who were ejected by the police, and similar scenes occurred when the play was later taken to America

JAMES JOYCE, DUBLINER

JAMES JOYCE (1882-1941) WAS PROBABLY THE MOST PARA-
DOXICAL FIGURE AMONG THE MANY IRISH WRITERS WHO
HAVE CHOSEN TO LEAVE THEIR NATIVE LAND.

Impatient with the provincial flavour of the literary revival and the constraints of Irish society, he spent most of his adult life on the Continent; his books are almost epitomes of European culture, filled with references to a dozen or more languages; and yet his most famous works are set in a Dublin which is described in intimate detail and is, on at least one level, their chief subject.

Like a surprising number of writers, Joyce was the son of a ne'er-do-well father whose embarrassments kept the family on the move. Joyce himself attended several Jesuit schools in

A SPELL IN THE TOWER. In 1903, just back in Dublin after nearly starving in Paris, Joyce moved into a Martello tower in Sandycove, then just outside the city. He shared the tower with the surgeon, writer and later politician Oliver St John Gogarty, on whom he based the character of Buck Mulligan in the equivalent episode at the beginning of *Ulysses*

Dublin and proved to be a brilliant student. By the time he graduated from University College in 1902 his literary promise was widely recognized, but he immediately left for Paris, where he lived in great poverty. Returning to Ireland when his mother was dying, he met a working girl, Nora Barnacle, who became his lifelong companion, although they did not marry until 1931. In October 1904 they left Ireland, in effect for good; Joyce worked as a language teacher in Trieste and Zurich until 1920, then settled in Paris, only returning to Zurich on the outbreak of the Second World War in 1939.

Apart from a volume of poems, Joyce's first book was *Dubliners*, a collection of short stories whose publication was delayed for nine years by censorship and other difficulties; written in a straightforward realistic style, the stories create a claustrophobic portrait of the city's society and hint at some of Joyce's central ideas. These emerge more clearly in *Portrait of the Artist as a Young Man* (1916), which contains much autobiographical material; the central character, Stephen Dedalus, finally rejects the Church, family and country to pursue his artistic vocation, using his chosen weapons of 'silence, exile and cunning'.

After writing a play, *Exiles*, Joyce completed what most readers regard as his masterpiece, *Ulysses*; in 1922 it was published in Paris, but it took fourteen years and a legal judgement before its candours became acceptable to the English-speaking world. Set in Dublin on a single day, it chronicles the doings of the Jewish advertising salesman Leopold Bloom, his wife Molly, and the young artist Stephen Dedalus. The action runs parallel with that of Homer's epic *The Odyssey*, to ironic effect. The time and viewpoint constantly shift, and there are dazzling linguistic effects culminating in Molly's interior monologue at the end of the book, an unpunctuated apparently spontaneous 'stream of consciousness'.

SILENCE, EXILE AND CUNNING WERE THE TACTICS DETERMINED UPON BY THE JOYCE-LIKE HERO OF PORTRAIT OF THE ARTIST AS A YOUNG MAN. JOYCE HIMSELF LEFT HIS NATIVE LAND FOR GOOD IN 1904; YET WHEN HE CAME TO CREATE A LITERARY MICROCOSM OF THE HUMAN WORLD IN ULYSSES, IT TOOK THE FORM OF HIS NATIVE DUBLIN

Joyce's final work, *Finnegans Wake* (1939), is an extraordinary, multi-layered, multi-lingual night-piece, representing the dreams of the saloon-keeper H. C. Earwicker and in effect comprising an allusive encyclopaedia of history, myth and culture; still controversial, it is variously seen as a dead end and as the climax of the European novel.

BREAKFAST AT BLOOM'S. IN JAMES JOYCE'S ULYSSES THE MAIN CHARACTER LEOPOLD BLOOM, BRINGS HIS WIFE MOLLY BREAKFAST IN BED AND THE DAYS POST. HERE, THEY ARE PLAYED BY MILO O'SHEA AND BARBARA JEFFORD IN THE 1967 FILM OF THE BOOK. THE DOMESTIC INTIMACY OF THE SCENE IS UNDERMINED BY THE FACT THAT MOLLY HAS A LETTER FROM HER LOVER, BLAZES BOYLAN UNDER HER PILLOW. BLOOM ASLO HAS EXTRA-MARITAL DESIGNS, REVEALED WHEN HE SETS OUT ON HIS ROUNDS. THE ENTIRE ACTION OF ULYSSES TAKES PLACE ON 16 JUNE 1904, NOW OFTEN CALLED 'BLOOMSDAY'

A LIVING TRADITION

ANY ACCOUNT OF EARLY 20TH-CENTURY LITERATURE IS INEVITABLY DOMINATED BY YEATS AND JOYCE, BUT THERE WERE MANY OTHER FINE IRISH WRITERS.

Fantasy and verbal play featured in novels such as James Stephen's *Crock of Gold* (1912) and Flann O'Brien's *At Swim-Two-Birds* (1939), while the Irish short-story tradition was carried on by Sean O'Faolain and Frank O'Connor. By contrast, two leading poets of the 1930s, C. Day-Lewis and Louis MacNeice, though Irish-born, did their most significant work in an English milieu.

Of an age with Day-Lewis and MacNeice, Samuel Beckett (1906-89) was widely recognized only in the 1950s, with the international success of his play *Waiting for Godot* (1952). Like James Joyce, who became his close friend, Beckett chose to live in exile while remaining intensely Irish. As if to go one better than Joyce, he wrote most of his early works in French, including the trilogy *Molloy, Malone Dies* and *The Unnameable* (1951-3), and *Godot* – all of which, however, he subsequently translated into an English sprinkled with Irish idioms.

Beckett's works are not set in any specific time and place, but deal with the human being stripped of the social and even sexual connections from which the personality is normally constructed. In *Godot*, on a stage that is bare except for a single tree, two men, Vladimir and Estragon, pass the time in talk as they wait for Godot – who never comes and, for all we know, does not exist. Apart from noisy interruptions by the blustering Pozzo and his servant Lucky, nothing happens and, implicitly, the same discussions and interruptions recur again and again. Despite the fundamental bleakness of Beckett's vision, his plays drew large audiences thanks to the clarity of his writing and the humorous side of his characters' fixations and dilemmas. *Endgame* (1957), *Krapp's Last Tape* (1958) and *Happy Days* (1961) were major theatrical events; but from the 1960s Beckett's work became increasingly concentrated, eventually consisting of only a few hundred words.

In 1969 Beckett became the third Irish writer (after Shaw and Yeats) to be awarded the Nobel Prize for Literature. The fourth and most recent laureate, the poet Seamus Heaney (1939-), is a popular and accessible writer whose reputation has steadily grown since the publication of his first collection, *Death of a Naturalist*, in 1966. His Nobel citation praises Heaney's poems for their 'lyrical beauty and ethical

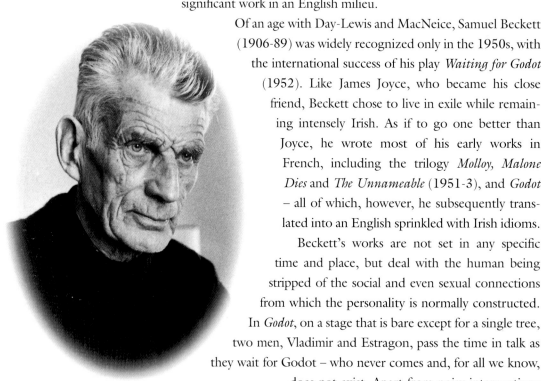

SAMUEL BECKETT seemed destined for a conventional academic career in Ireland, but gave it up to live in France. His writings suggest a man self-absorbed in contemplating the bleakness of existence, yet during the Second World War he worked for the Resistance, and was awarded the Croix de Guerre. In the 1950s, his play *Waiting for Godot* made him famous

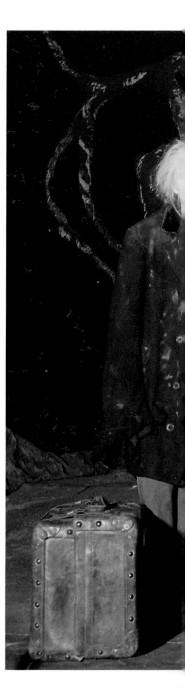

depth, which exalt everyday miracles and the living past'; born into a Catholic family in Northern Ireland, his work inevitably reflects experiences of bigotry and violence, but he has never been in any propagandist sense a political poet.

The many other gifted figures on the contemporary scene include Brian Friel (1929-), author of such critically acclaimed plays as *Translations* (1970) and *Dancing at Lughnasa* (1990), the poets Tom Paulin, Paul Durcan and Eavan Boland, and a galaxy of novelists and short-story writers, among them Edna O'Brien, William Trevor and Roddy Doyle.

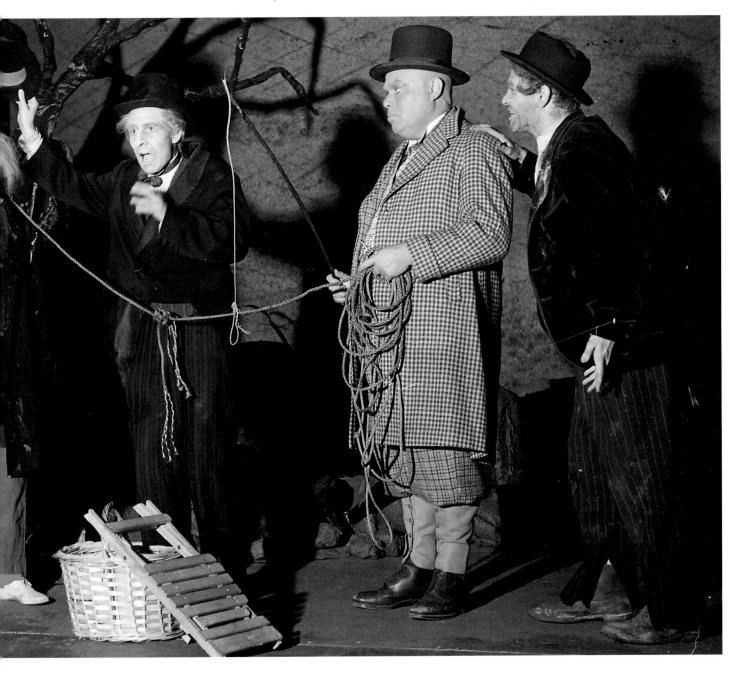

STILL WAITING. A 1955 performance of *Waiting for Godot* with (left to right) Timothy Bateson as Lucky, Hugh Burden as Vladimir, Peter Bull as Pozzo, and Peter Woodthorpe as Estragon. Vladimir and Estragon talk, propose course of action, and do nothing; Pozzo and Lucky play out the roles of bully and slave; Godot. . . keeps them waiting

CONTEMPORARY IRELAND

LEFT: The city centre, Dublin, bisected by the river liffey
RIGHT: Foley's public house on Merrion Row, Dublin.

JAMES JOYCE LOOKS OUT ON O'CONNELL STREET

ALTHOUGH DEEPLY CONSCIOUS OF THEIR PAST,
THE IRISH HAVE COME TO TERMS WITH
THE MODERN WORLD. IN THE FUTURE THEIR
BUOYANCY AND CREATIVE ENERGY SEEM
TO ASSURE THEM A PROMINENT PLACE IN
EUROPE AND THE WORLD

TRADITION & CHANGE

UP UNTIL THE 1960S, IRELAND WAS A COUNTRY WHERE CHANGE WAS REJECTED IN FAVOUR OF TRADITIONAL PATTERNS OF LIFE AND OLD ALLEGIANCES. IN THE REPUBLIC OF IRELAND IN THE SOUTH, THE MAIN POLITICAL PARTIES HAD THEIR ORIGINS IN THE CIVIL WAR BETWEEN THE PRO- AND ANTI-TREATY FACTIONS.

Fine Gael ('Tribe of Gael') was directly descended from the political leadership which had accepted Partition in 1922 and had subsequently won the Civil War; while the Fianna Fail ('Soldiers of Destiny') party was the creation of the rejectionist chief Eamon De Valera.

LOOKING BACK. IN NORTHERN IRELAND, COMMUNITY MEMORIES ARE LONG AND OLD BATTLES ARE REGULARLY RE-FOUGHT. ON THIS LOYALIST MURAL IN BELFAST, KING BILLY CROSSES THE BOYNE ONCE MORE, AND ONCE MORE LAYS LOW HIS ENEMIES AND MAKES IRELAND SAFE FOR PROTESTANTISM

Despite the outcome of the Civil War, it was the austere figure of Eamon de Valera who dominated the political scene from the early 1930s. Dedicated to preserving a completely self-sufficient, essentially rural, devoutly Catholic Ireland, he adopted policies that protected Irish producers – and Irish values – from

foreign competition and unfamiliar ideas. This was an unworldly, doubtless nobly motivated programme, but the price was high. Ireland remained a very poor country (and not all the poverty was of the merely 'frugal' sort that De Valera held to be acceptable and even praiseworthy); the numbers leaving to find new lives overseas continued to be high; and the rest of the world viewed Ireland as a backwater. But in Ireland itself De Valera's vision was not seriously challenged until after he retired as taoiseach in 1959 and took on the non-political role of president.

His successor in the premiership was Sean Lemass. By the time he took office, Lemass had been a follower of De Valera and a Fianna Fail loyalist for more than a quarter of a century. But as taoiseach he set out on a fresh course, encouraging the development of new industries and large-scale foreign investment, while starting to lower the tariff barriers that discriminated against foreign products. Lemass's policies brought a rapid improvement in the Irish standard of living and, for better or for worse, raised the spectres of materialism and consumerism that De Valera had tried to keep at bay. The likelihood of a return to De Valera's values became increasingly remote when television entered Irish homes. At first this happened via British programmes which could be picked up by sets in the Republic; then, from 1962, a national service was inaugurated by Radio Telefis Eireann.

The next stage in the modernization of the Republic occurred in 1973, when Lemass's successor, Jack Lynch, successfully applied for Irish membership of the European Community (EC: now the European Union or EU). By the early 1970s it was apparent that new social and economic conditions were altering Irish attitudes. And not necessarily for the worse: observers noted that, while still proud of their heritage, the Irish had become more future-oriented and less obsessed with old antagonisms and grievances.

THE REPUBLIC'S PARLIAMENT has conducted its business in the appropriately dignified setting of Leinster House since 1922; Parliament, the Oireachtas, consists of a lower house, the Dail, and the patrician Senate. Leinster House (1745) was designed by Richard Cassels. Between 1815 and 1822 it housed the Royal Dublin Society, which made it the centre of a cultural complex including the National Library and the National Museum

ALSO LOOKING BACK. MURALS PAINTED ON THE SIDES OF HOUSES REPRESENT AN ART FORM USED BY BOTH NORTHERN IRISH COMMUNITIES. THIS NATIONALIST EXAMPLE, FROM BELFAST, EMPHASIZES THE HARDSHIPS EXPERIENCED BY THE OPPRESSED PEASANTRY

In Northern Ireland, as in the Republic, there were few serious challenges to the established order until the 1960s. Power lay with the Protestant and Unionist majority, exercised through the province's government at Stormont Castle. The large Catholic minority, discriminated against in politics, jobs, housing and education, felt helpless in the face of intimidation by the security forces, and the only group prepared to oppose 'Stormont' was the paramilitary IRA, which aimed to overthrow the state by violence. The IRA, or Irish Republican Army, took its title from the forces which had resisted the British in 1919-21; but its campaigns attracted little grass-roots support among Northern Catholics and had petered out by the late 1950s.

The radical idealism and rising expectations of the 1960s led to the emergence of a different type of agitation, the civil rights movement of 1968. Unlike the IRA, this was not designed to subvert the state and end partition, but to secure equal rights for all – which in practice meant for the Catholic minority. Marches and other forms of legal agitation highlighted the injustices of the Stormont system and attracted international attention and sympathy. For a time, peaceful change seemed a possibility, but the intractable and often violent Protestant response led to counter-violence and rioting; the IRA reappeared as the protector of the threatened Catholic community; British troops were sent to the province in an attempt to preserve law and order; direct rule from Westminster replaced the Stormont regime; and with the founding of Loyalist (Protestant) paramilitary groups, headline-making terrorist acts were regularly perpetrated in the name of both communities.

Over the following two decades, no solution looked like working; this applied equally to tough government measures such as internment without trial, to an experiment in 'power-sharing' between the two communities, and to the 'Round Table' talks of 1991-2. Meanwhile there were IRA bombings in Britain and on the Continent; but much more extensive damage was done, by paramilitaries on both sides, in the North. The destruction was accompanied by the 'ghettoization' of Belfast and Dublin, where mixed communities effectively ceased to exist, and by Mafia-style activity on the part of the paramilitaries, who financed their activities by protection rackets and administered their own brand of summary justice to criminals and suspected informers.

MAKING IT NEW HAS TAKEN ON A DIFFERENT MEANING AS FAR AS SOME AREAS OF DUBLIN ARE CONCERNED. THE TEMPLE BAR AREA, WITH ITS NARROW STREETS AND OLD HOUSES, WAS ONCE SCHEDULED FOR DEMOLITION AND REDEVELOPMENT. FORTUNATELY THE CITY FATHERS REALIZED IN TIME THAT PEOPLE ACTUALLY LIKED THE INTIMATE ATMOSPHERE OF SUCH OLD QUARTERS, AND IT HAS BEEN MADE OVER INTO AN ARTY AREA THAT ATTRACTS BOTH DUBLINERS AND VISITORS, WITH A MIX OF GALLERIES, BOOKSHOPS, DESIGN AND THEATRE PROJECTS, SMALL HOTELS, CAFÉ-BARS AND ETHNIC RESTAURANTS

But there were also some positive developments. The British and Irish governments co-operated increasingly closely. Much of the damage caused by terrorism was made good with surprising speed, and British subsidies and aid from the EU and international organizations created a surprisingly robust, if patchy, prosperity. Direct rule brought an end to the worst abuses of the Stormont era. Outside the worst trouble-spots, life went on much as usual and the people of the North remained remarkably energetic and cheerful. Though fundamental attitudes hardly seemed to soften, there was a general longing for peace that expressed itself in joyful celebrations at the announcement in August 1994 of an IRA ceasefire, adhered to a few weeks later by the Loyalist paramilitaries. Its fragility was shown when it broke down in 1996; but its renewal the following year gave fresh grounds for hope.

SALON IN SPLENDOUR. THE CROWN IS ONE OF THE BEST-KNOWN BELFAST LANDMARKS, FOR VISUAL AS WELL AS ALCOHOLIC REASONS. NORTH OR SOUTH, THE IRISH ARE A CONVIVIAL PEOPLE WHOSE PUBLIC HOUSES ARE CENTRES OF WITTY DISCOURSE AND ENTERTAINMENT. BUT CONTRARY TO POPULAR OPINION, THE IRISH ARE NOT PARTICULARLY HEAVY DRINKERS, AND THE TEMPERANCE MOVEMENT HAS A LARGE FOLLOWING

MODERN SHOPPING, FOR MANY PEOPLE, MEANS DOZENS OF OUTLETS CONCENTRATED IN ONE LARGE STRUCTURE MADE OF GLASS, STEEL AND CONCRETE; AND IRELAND IS NO EXCEPTION. THE EDIFICE ABOVE IS CASTLE COURT SHOPPING CENTRE IN BELFAST

Since the 1960s, the Republic of Ireland has benefited from its participation in a dynamic world economy, and has rapidly narrowed the gap in living standards between it and its European neighbours. By most accepted econometric criteria, Irish society has made tremendous, undeniable advances. It has also, inevitably, experienced the negative side of modernity: a roller-coaster economy in which boom and bust alternate; chronic job insecurity and the seemingly intractable phenomenon of high unemployment, especially distressing in a country with a remarkably young population; and the related problems of crime, drug abuse and alienation.

These are difficulties experienced by all modern societies, and Ireland, like the rest, will have to solve them or else learn to live with them. But extra strains have been caused by the struggle of ideas that has been another feature of the country's opening up to the outside world. Traditional roles have been modified, most spectacularly in 1990, when a woman, Mary Robinson, was elected President of Ireland. And the attitude of society and the state towards private moral behaviour has become more liberal, despite opposition from a highly conservative Church establishment. A landmark event, following a referendum in favour, was the first statutory provision for divorce in 1995; and equally significant was the fact that Bertie Aherne, leader of Fianna Fail, was able to become taoiseach in 1997 although he was separated from his wife and cohabiting with another woman. It should also be added that the Republic remains devoutly Catholic – arguably, by most statistical tests, the most devout country in the whole of Europe. And the huge numbers of pilgrims who now converge on Knock in Mayo, thanks to the proximity of an international airport indicate that not all the advantages of modernity are merely secular.

Modern culture and modern consumer goods are cosmopolitan (though most often perceived as American), spreading everywhere by appealing successfully to convenience and fashion. The Irish, like other peoples with strong traditions, have been worried by the possible threat that this poses to their identity. Paradoxically, tourism is both part of the problem and a major industry that every Irish government is keen to encourage, using 'Irishness' as the bait to bring in business. Consequently Ireland has turned into a land of 'heritage' attractions and 'experiences', from medieval banquets at Bunratty and other castles to exhibitions such as the Queenstown Story at Cobh, dwelling on past injustices.

PEDESTRIAN PLEASURES ARE NOW PART OF IRISH LIFE. GRAFTON STREET HAS BEEN ENTIRELY CLEARED OF TRAFFIC, ENABLING STROLLERS TO WINDOW-SHOP OR BROWSE IN BIG STORES SUCH AS WEIR'S THE JEWELLER'S OR BROWN THOMAS THE HABERDASHER'S, FOLLOWING UP WITH A SESSION IN ONE OF THE WELL-KNOWN BEWLEY'S ORIENTAL CAFÉS

Whatever the merits (or demerits) of heritage events, living traditions must be more important. Modernity has not yet sapped Irish hospitality and friendliness, and at the moment there is still a pleasant contrast between the leisurely pace of life in the countryside and the energy characteristic of the big city. The landscape and the climate are essentially unchanged. And outside influences seem to be nourishing rather than destroying distinctively Irish culture, to judge from the books, plays, films, bands and dances which are not only created in Ireland but are winning international reputations. There has never been anywhere quite like Ireland, and it seems unlikely that Ireland will ever become quite like anywhere else.

INDEX

ACKNOWLEDGMENTS

AKG LONDON 74, /Keith Collie 120, 120-121, /Hugh Lane Municipal Gallery, Dublin 143 top, /National Museum of Ireland 25, 88-89, /Michael Teller 115, 119 BODLEIAN LIBRARY /MS Laud misc. 720 pt II f.226v 58, /MS Laud misc. 720 pt II f.232 49 left, /Ms Laud misc.610 f.59 131, /MS Laud misc.720 pt II f.226 50 BRIDGEMAN ART LIBRARY /Agnew & Sons 56 right, /British Library 26, 62, /Bonham's 55 right, /Bradford Art Galleries & Museums 100 right, /Christie's 52-53, 82 botttom, /Crawford Municipal Art Gallery, Cork 102, /Fine Art Society, London 101, /Fine-Lines (Fine Art), Warwickshire 98-99, /Philip Mould, Historical Portraits Ltd 132, /Private Collections 26-27, 32, 55 left, 103 bottom, 135, 139, /Sheffield City Art Gallery 100 left, /Victoria & Albert Museum 96 top, 96 bottom, 126-127 BRITISH MUSEUM 45 CHRISTIE'S IMAGES 30-31, 82-83 CORBIS UK LTD 39, /Tom Bean 20-21, 22-23, /Dave Houser 108, /Library of Congress 41, /Gianni Dagli Orti 28 C.M. DIXON 18 top, 18 bottom, 20, 24 left, 48, 82 top, 85 bottom, 106, 107, 108-109, 114-115, 130-131 E.T. ARCHIVE 52, 57, /Imperial War Museum 37, /Victoria & Albert Museum 96-97 MARY EVANS PICTURE LIBRARY 17, 36, 38, 64-65 top, 72 left, 81 top, 81 bottom FINE ART PHOTOGRAPHS 60-61 top, 60-61 bottom, 66-67, 67, /By courtesy of Fine Art of Oakhan 104-105, /By Courtesy of Gavin Graham Gallery, London W11 71 WERNER FORMAN ARCHIVE 78-79 top, 86, 130, /National Museum of Ireland 46, 47, 86-87, 87 RAY GARDNER 24 right, 133, 134-135 ROBERT HARDING PICTURE LIBRARY /Philip Craven 123, /Gavin Heller 128-129, /Michael Jenner 44, /Roy Rainford 19, 70, 88, /Adam Woolfitt 44-45, 84 HULTON GETTY PICTURE COLLECTION jacket front top left, 31, 34, 34-35, 35, 36-37, 38-39, 40, 40-41, 42 top, 56 left, 58-59, 59, 60, 62-63, 64, 103 top, 105, 129, 140 top, 145 top, 146 IMAGES COLOUR LIBRARY LTD jacket back flap, 8, 10, 13 top, 42 bottom, 70-71 IMAGE IRELAND 63, 152-153, /Tom Ennis 11, /Errol Forbes 8-9, 10-11, 15, 16-17, /Brian Hughes 64-65 bottom, /Bill Kirk 150-151, 154 left, /Alain Le Garsmeur 3, 27, 42-43, 76-77, 77, 78-79 bottom, 110-111 bottom, 111, 112-113, 121, 124-125, 125, 128, 140 bottom, 144, 148-149, 150, /James McEvoy 7 top, /John Scovill 12-13, /Geray Sweeeney 104, 108-109, 114, 118-119 NORMA JOSEPH 4, 13 bottom, 119, 127 A.F. KERSTING 99, 122 KOBAL COLLECTION 145 bottom LEEDS MUSEUMS & GALLERIES /Lotherton Hall 32-33 MANDER & MITCHENSON 78, 134, 138-139, 140-141, 142, 143 bottom, 146-147 MOLYNEUX ASSOCIATES jacket front top right, 113 NATIONAL MUSEUM OF IRELAND 49 right, 72 right, 74-75, 85 top, 89, 90, 92-93, 94, 94-95, 95 REDFERNS /Brian Shuel 69, /Brigitte Engl 68-69 REED INTERNATIONAL BOOKS LTD 28-29, 50-51, 54, 68, 75, 76, 132-133, 136, 136-137, 137, 138, /Trinity College Library, Dublin 90-91, 91, 92, 94 PETER RYAN 148 NEIL SETCHFIELD 126, 149, 151, 152, 155 right TONY STONE IMAGES jacket front bottom, jacket back, 7 bottom, 9,14, 14-15, 80, 116-117 DON SUTTON INTERNATIONAL PHOTO LIBRARY 73, 106-107, 110-111 top, 116, 122-123, 124 UNIVERSIT TSBIBLIOTHEK HEIDELBERG 23 ULSTER MUSEUM, BELFAST Photograph © Ulster Museum, Belfast, reproduced with kind permission of theTrustees 16